Mustn't Grumble

Comic & Tragic Verses

Andy Fawthrop

ISBN-10:153686627X
ISBN-13:978-1536866278

DEDICATION

This collection of poetry, verse, doggerel, or whatever you'd like to call it, is dedicated to those few brave souls who first encouraged me to write, and then to perform, the contents. I'd also like to thank them for not running away, smiling bravely, and lying through their teeth to assure me that they'd really enjoyed the results. You know who are, and I thank you from the bottom of my bewildered heart.

MUSTN'T GRUMBLE

If you hail from "Up North", the Northern part of England that is, you'll be familiar with this phrase. "Mustn't Grumble" is one of the stock answers to the question "Awreet?" It's what passes for a normal greeting between northern folks. The person asking has no real interest in the health of the other, and the person being asked is polite enough not to answer in any detail whatsoever. Just for reference, the other stock (acceptable) answers are "Fair To Middling" and "Champion", although the latter is possibly a little boastful and may lead to an actual conversation. "Mustn't Grumble" simply means "I'm OK, now let's talk about something (anything) else".

Bill Underwood
2021

MUSTN'T GRUMBLE

COMIC & TRAGIC VERSES

Many a true word is spoken in jest

GROWING OLDER

You simply weren't going to grow older. Life was going to be one long adventure stretching off into the far distance. You would never reach the grand old age of 50, or 60, or 70. You weren't ever going to be a crumbly, or a crustie…or – hang on just a second! – what the hell happened? All of a sudden something changed. One minute you were looking *up* the road to see what was ahead, and the next minute you were looking back *down* the road to find out where you'd been! When, exactly, did you cross The Great Divide?

With greater age comes experience, perspective, a sense of proportion, maturity and serenity. And aches and pains, grumpiness, anger, and a general sense of bewilderment. So welcome to my world. Join me in my journey as an honorary Grumpy Old Git and Curmudgeon. I find that laughter is the best possible response to most things. It stops me from killing my Fellow Man.

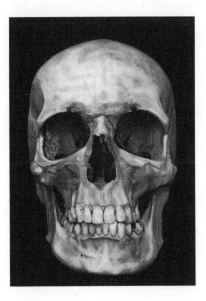

Manopause

I thought I'd better get on and take action,
to counter the loss of libido and sterility,
between my mid-life and Alzheimers,
and to get back some signs of virility.

So now I'm a Man Behaving Badly,
re-stating what it is to be male -
I've started learning guitar and the uke,
and I'm growing hair for my pony-tail.

The mountain-bike is on order and,
'cause I don't want to look like a Charley,
I'm going to get me a motor-bike,
which (what else?), must be a Harley.

That's what I'll ride in good weather,
but I'll need something cooler (of course!),
so I've been round to the dealers,
and I'll soon be driving my Porsche.

I'm having my ear piercing tomorrow,
to show you all that I'm one of the few,
and to complete the picture,
next week I'm getting a lurid tattoo.

Then I'll wear my baseball cap with pride,
pulling it down low over my eyelids.
(I might have to get some work done there,
but I'm determined to get down with the kids).

You see it's not all testosterone and Viagra,
and I say this without any compunction,
there's other ways than hormone treatment
to ward off erectile dysfunction.

No – the hot flushes and flashes,
the irritability and mood-changes can wait -
there's a lot more to be worried about,
like the parlous state of my prostate.

I may be losing my hair and my marbles,
gradual decline may be a part of the story,
but I'm determined to hang on to my manhood,
and go out in a grand blaze of glory.

You see some of it may be biological,
but it's psychological, to tell you the truth,
I'm a grumpy old man, sporting a fake tan,
and I'm trying to hang on to my youth.

So you can all look at me and laugh,
as you sit there with your slack jaws,
but I won't be the one who's declining –
I'm off to defeat the Manopause.

Waterworld

Who turned on the water-works?
and left the nasal tap
running and dripping
ithe middle of my face?
It seems the flow is never-ending,
a steady stream of liquid
pouring from my puffy eyes
and dropping from my nose
into crumpled handkerchiefs and tissues

Who made the view so bleary,
unclear and smeary?
The blubbing and the blabbing,
dabbing and wiping
through the sneezing
wheezing in the throat

Drowning in a soggy world
sometimes gushing in a torrent
then slowing to a gentle leaking
in this wet and watery world
of pollen-polluted nostrils
in a hot and fevered face
that can only find relief
buried deep within a pillow

The O-word

My medical was a total disaster:
the doctor's face turned rather grim.
It was a big fail, when I got on the scale,
and he said: "you're not very slim!"
"There's no good way I can tell you this,
although you might get yourself in a sulk.
It seems it's your fate, to be hugely overweight:
you're the size of The Incredible Hulk.
I've tried being subtle, I've tried being coy,
there seems no way I can get through.
Perhaps invective can be more effective
I don't know what else I can do!"

Then he let me have it with both barrels:
"You're big, you're burly, you're chubby,
with more avoir-dupois than average,
you're chunky, not hunky, definitely tubby.
You're full-faced, fat, floppy and fleshy,
a big lard-arse, and as large as a barge.
You're not finely honed, not merely big-boned,
you're a roly-poly, a great tub of marge.
Your size is….. amplitudinous,
a chump with a bump, plus a huge rump,
a chubster, a big rounded tubster, like a partridge,
My God but you're plump!"

Sadly I looked down at my vanishing waist,
and said "why do you use words such as these?
Just what is it you're trying to tell me?
Are you saying that I may be obese?"
The doctor was completely taken aback,
so he scowled, and he looked at me hard.
Then he said "you're not listening, are you?
You king-sized great tub of lard!
I'm obviously not making myself clear.
Let's say that you're of voluminous size,
Falstaffian, Brobdignagian,
it's quite clear who ate all the pies!"

"Your expansive capaciousness
goes beyond any known bound.
You're beefy and burly, fudgy and pudgy,
and it's years since you last saw the ground!
Gargantuan, elephantine and mammoth
are three words that may easily vex,
but they hold no candle, to your love handles,
or the scale of your Body Mass Index.
You must eat less, and exercise more,
it's time to take a clinical stand,
it's time to realise that a balanced diet
does not mean a burger in each hand!"

"Your massive, mountainous diet must cease:
no more chocolate or cream or fruit jellies,
nor guacamole dips, nor fish and chips,
until you've got rid of those bellies!
It's calorie-counting from here onwards:
you must drain yourself to the dregs.
You can't make a much thinner omelette,
without breaking low-cholesterol eggs!"
At last the light was beginning to dawn:
I could see what he was trying to state,
so I just asked him to clarify:
"Here - are you saying that I'm over-weight?"

That Old Toothless Dog *(or the thin end of the wedge)*

Here we are again, as you lie on the floor,
at the side of my chair, your lead all slack.
No wonder, by the look of you,
we were asked to sit at the back.

I felt it was the least that we could do,
because you're not too strong in the knees.
For they didn't want the other pets put out,
nor frightened, nor infected with fleas.

Your coat's all matted and tangled,
and I didn't feel that I could quibble.
For it's quite obvious wherever we sit,
there's going to be lots of your dribble.

Cos now you're old, and you're toothless,
you're half-deaf and you're half-blind,
all of which I can put up with:
it's the incontinence that I mind.

It's hard to list all of your ailments,
it's hard to know just where to start,
but I guess your principal problem
is quite how often you fart.

You get in the way wherever you flop down,
you cost us a fortune in dog food.
You can't seem to leave anything alone,
and when we get home, we find everything chewed.

You're becoming increasingly forgetful,
you just look puzzled, you old wretch,
'cos you stop half way to the stick:
you've forgotten what you were going to fetch.

You've become a useless guard-dog:
the burglars can't believe their luck.
Your toothless jaws can no longer bite them,
only give them a quite nasty suck.

You don't bark in time to warn us,
they're upon us all too soon,
and then, when there's *no* danger,
you spend hours howling at the moon.

You've become an economic burden,
and now that you're not very well,
you're neither use nor ornament,
and on top of all that, you smell.

So here we are for your last journey,
the end of the road for you as a pet.
The life-force of you will soon be ended,
by that needle in the hands of the vet.

So don't you look up at me like that,
with those big, brown, cloudy but trusting eyes.
I'm sure you can see into my purpose,
that this visit's one way can't be disguised.

You've grown up with me and the children,
you've always been faithful and loyal.
You've put in your years of good service,
and to us you've been a friend quite royal.

You've become part of the family,
as if you were related by blood.
We couldn't take on a new puppy now:
I just don't think that we could.

Dammit, everybody loves you,
though you're a toothless old hound.
You're just a part of the furniture –
think that it's time we turned round.

Let's leave this deathly waiting room,
let's walk right out calm and steady.
You don't need to be pushed along,
 you can do this when you're good and ready

For now that it's come right down to it,
I find that I can't just erase yer.
We'll be doing it to people next,
and that's the road to euthanasia!

9

Senior Escorts Ltd *(or my secret life as an aging hooker)*

I get my assignments from the agency –
there's quite a few of us on the books.
I'm working for Twilight Escorts -
for I still haven't lost all of my looks.
I'm what they call a Silver Stallion,
serving older ladies, with a quick wink.
You might have thought they were past it,
but there's more call for it than you might think.

I specialise in the older clientele:
crusties, crumblies and old wrecks.
I'm not worried about their ages,
as long as they'll pay me for sex.
For everyone has needs to be met,
and if I can speak to you frankly,
there are worse ways to spend your afternoons,
than providing some hanky-panky.

For elderly widows get lonely,
and just want to have some fun days,
but I think that it also helps,
we do pensioner discounts on Mondays.
I can only handle one or two jobs in a day,
but it's not the energy that I lack.
I just have to be quite careful,
or else I'll put out my back.

My ladies have simple requirements,
and don't make complex conditions.
I'm not quite as lithe as I was,
and don't do funny positions.
I'm clean and I travel quite light,
and I'm one of their younger boys.
I don't need much equipment:
just baby-oil and one or two sex toys.

Afternoon is the most popular time,
and I know that it sounds corny,
but it's when the clients are mostly awake,
as well as feeling most horny.

So, after I've parked my Zimmer frame in the hall,
and perhaps been offered a medicinal whiskey,
it's time to get on with the business,
and chase her round the house, if she's frisky.

It's all straight-forward once in the bedroom,
and I'm certainly not mocking.
I'm quite used to false teeth and false limbs,
and rolling down their surgical stockings.
Medical appliances hold no fear for me,
and I'll also help with suspenders,
and afterwards we'll share a cup of Sanatogen,
and settle down watching Eastenders.

But I can't stay for too long at their house,
even though they might make a fuss.
I can't drive any longer at my age,
and I have to go and catch the last bus.
I've got my regular customers,
but the flow is hardly a Niagara.
Still - my doctor's quite understanding,
and keeps me supplied with Viagra.

I provide a reliable service,
and it's one I think that appeals:
for my latest advertising slogan,
I'm selling myself as "Feels on Wheels".
We're sponsored by Help The Randy,
and other organisations you'll learn.
Our latest out-sourcing contract
is in support of Urge Concern.

Satisfaction's not guaranteed,
I feel I just ought to mention,
but what better way can you think of
to fritter away most of your pension?
So if you're in need of my services,
and we cater for all sorts of ages,
log on to our website at once,
or look for us in Yellow Pages.

Hair Today, Gone Tomorrow

We need to talk about hair
The stuff that covers the human body
The stuff that everyone knows
From the tops of our heads to (in some cases) the tops of our toes
That's how it generally goes
Yes, we need to talk about hair
The stuff that can be dark or oftentimes fair
Of how it goes in a cycle through life
With little to start with when we're born
Then growing and sprouting and flourishing
So we spend fortunes on shampoos
And conditioners for nourishing
Cutting and styling and shaping
Plucking and singeing and shaving
We've developed the knack
For back, sack and crack
A devious desire to dazzle
Perhaps even a cheeky vajazzle
In an orgy of depilation
A whole industry that's addressing
Our copious needs for hair-dressing

But that's only the upward trajectory
Of hair's growth and our vanity
Before the onset of insanity
As towards old age we're spinning
When fading and falling and thinning
Create a look that's no longer winning
But that's what happens up on the head
You start losing it faster instead
And also down there below
You'll find it's starting to go

But there's an exception to this general moulting
That some find personally revolting
When the orifices of the head
Start to take over instead
For there can be no doubting
About the range of new sprouting
A new flourishing that fills

The eyebrows, the ears and the nostrils
But I'm willing to bet
It's not finished yet
It's just the same hair that you get
Simply looking for a new outlet

Fifty Sheds Of Grey

A man has to have some hobbies in life,
Something that'll make him leap out of bed,
And, when he arrives at a certain age,
That *something* tends to be a grey shed.

It's funny - they never appeal in anyone's youth,
When things tend to happen all in a deluge,
But once you've been married a few years,
A shed can be a man's haven, or refuge.

It doesn't take much – a shed can be quite modest,
A roof, a window, and four wooden walls:
Just somewhere homely to escape to,
Whenever an unwelcome chore calls.

It's a manly or masculine thing,
Just to get yourself behind a closed door,
To rummage around in the darkness,
And to spread your things out on the floor.

For in this exclusive, men-only club,
You need never ask anyone's pardon,
Just to disappear down the primrose path,
To your shed, at the end of the garden.

Yes, a shed can be a man's very own kingdom,
The realm where what he says is what goes:
A place to play with his bits and pieces,
And what he does inside – nobody knows.

And he can make the place quite homely,
Then spread out as much as he dare,
By getting a radio, perhaps, and some carpet,
And, if there's room, a comfortable chair.

A bottle or two and a few glasses,
And an optic can easily form up a bar.
Then he can get all of his mates round,
And be the gardeners' idea of a star.

You see it becomes *more* than a shelter -
It's not just for keeping out of the rain -
It's a sanctuary that's out of the house,
A place that might keep a man sane.

So, don't denigrate such constructions,
And pay heed to what I've just said,
For a man's the king of his castle,
When he's finally alone, in his own shed.

Cough

There's something that I need to get off my chest
For I'm feeling rather queasy
And my breathing's gone all wheezy
I reckon I'm scoring about a seven
On the International scale
The Cough Index of Looseness
I don't think there's any question
That I've got some bronchial congestion
And I need to make a major contribution
To the UK Phlegm and Mucus Depository
This soothing menthol mixture
May become a bedside fixture
This special fruit and honey syrup
Has made me Expectorant of a cure
For it's the thing that Linctus together

Beige

As I get to be another year older,
I think I'm starting to change.
My taste has gone right out of the window
In a way that seems spooky and strange.
It all began with magnolia;
other paint colours just seemed to gawp.
I could no longer stand any bright shades,
and I developed a fondness for taupe.

I believe that it's a rite of passage,
one you reach at a certain age.
Everything else appears far too jazzy,
and you get your first craving for beige.
It used to be brown, the colour of ear-wax,
but the appeal of that tint's started to fade.
What I was really looking for, I realised,
was something matched to my hearing-aid.

It's the same thing with clothing –
attractive material now makes me retch.
I find I'm shopping for easy-care fabrics,
and trousers with waistbands that stretch.
"No-iron", and "Sta-prest" things that are cosy,
and easy-clean, so long as they're not green.
Slacks, wind-cheaters and cardigans,
in a nice Polyester, or in Crimpelene.

I'm becoming an old person, I think,
I'm obviously reaching that stage,
Where I don't care anymore what things look like,
but it's more important to be beige.
I crave a jacket with leather elbow patches,
and trousers with vents and with slants,
anything that will hide the volume,
and the shape of my incontinence pants.

I'm not looking for sex, but my reading specs;
with bright colours I'm near sated,
And it's no longer the style, but the comfort,
which is why everything I wear's elasticated.

I'd rather be dead, than wear anything red:
in fact that would drive me to rage,
and I wouldn't feel mellow, dressed up in yellow;
no – the only thing that'll do now is beige.

I'd put up a fight, never to wear white;
the loss of the rainbow I'm not going to rue.
I'm just same about purple or black,
and don't even mention royal blue!
No – it's time to accept that time has moved on,
my taste has declined, and I've turned over a page.
So you can keep all shades and variations –
there's only one colour for me now – and it's beige.

Health, wealth and happiness: *(or how I was persuaded to seek health and youth, but gave it all up for booze and fags)*

Now I'm the first to admit,
although I'm certainly not wealthy,
I'd like to try and live as long as I can,
and that includes being healthy.
My other half – she looked hard at me,
and cast her critical eye.
"You need to get into shape" she said,
"and here are some ideas you can try".

She reeled off a number of therapies:
in fact she became quite verbal.
They were mostly New Age and Modern:
some were Chinese and some were herbal.
I started on aroma therapy,
which created a wonderful smell.
but that just made me sleepy,
and off the treatment table I fell.

So nursing some bumps and some bruises,
I went to see a chiropractor.
She caused me so much pain that I cried,
and I'm afraid that I then sacked her.
So seeking for calmer approaches,
I tried ayurvedic head massage.
It brought a smile to my lips,
and peace to my ugly visage.

Hypnotherapy, meditation and yoga,
and various types of new diet:
wheat-free, dairy-free and Atkins –
if it was faddy, I just had to try it.
Reflexology, and ear candling,
and all sorts of new medication.
Then finally I built myself up
to try Transcendental Meditation.

This led to a new feeling of calmness:
my chakras were all in a line.
I started to feel so much better:
in fact I felt really quite fine.

And this was all very well for a while,
but it merely calmed my mental state:
I needed something else for my body –
a new person I wanted to create.

So I started to become more ambitious:
it's what you do at such a juncture -
manipulation, electro-therapy,
and finally some acupuncture.
With needles all over my body,
my wellness began to increase.
If I could just push to the next stage –
well – wonders might never cease.

I looked out for more treatments:
anything health-like related.
Until finally I succumbed,
and had my colon irrigated.
It's called hydro-therapy,
but there's no need to sob -
it was all quite pleasant really,
and much easier than my later boob-job.

For I'd become addicted to nips and to tucks:
I didn't need to be urged on.
I was even getting a discount
from my cosmetic surgeon.
But I suppose it's the human condition,
to look for something more exotic,
when your diet gets increasingly boring,
and everything's become pro-biotic.

Then finally the treatments stopped working:
what was once tight now only sags.
Anyway I've discovered a new diet:
it consists of chips, of beer and of fags.
So let this story become a warning to you:
don't think you can make yourself healthy.
Just stick with what you know,
and that way you might keep yourself wealthy.

I Remember What's-Her-Name

I was only thinking just the other day
About many things so far away
Before my recollection could wane
As I took a trip down Memory Lane
That I hadn't seen her for such a long time
The girl I had courted back in my prime
She was handsome, and she was pretty
She lived in old Bradford City
I was sweet on her, which she surely knew
And I think that she was sweet on me too
So many years have now slipped by
How the decades have tended to fly
Such a long time since I played the courtship game....
I wonder whatever happened to... What's-Her-Name?

After such a promising start
We gradually drifted apart
Then came that fateful day
When her family moved far away
We saw each other for one final night
Of course we promised we'd write
It didn't happen and, as is often the case,
I think she got married to... What's-His-Face
And as the story usually bids
There followed at least a couple of kids
Then, just like you read in the books
She faded, and lost all of her looks

Now I wish I hadn't so tarried
She was the girl I ought to have married
But I'll never know whether
We might have been happy together
You know - right after our first date
I *knew* she was my soul-mate
So close that our spirits were linking
We knew what each other was thinking
It's such a shame it didn't last
And now it's all so far in the past
I don't think either of us was to blame...
I just wish I could remember her bloody name!

Radioactive

I've had this little operation,
On the theatre table laid prostrate,
They've fixed me up, and I'm good to go,
Now they've irradiated my prostate.

Yes they treated me with radiation,
With hundreds of tiny little seeds,
Now I'm full of alpha particles,
That will soon provide for all my needs.

I've got my own internal power source,
Which is a most important factor.
Now I'm a little generator,
Like a tiny nuclear reactor.

This fusion makes me glow in the dark,
Just like the ad with the Reddy-Brek kid,
And if the nation gets short of power,
They'll just connect me to the National Grid.

Now you'll see I've got a new demeanour,
That there's a special quality to my gaze:
It comes from a sense of inner power –
Well - that and I'm transmitting gamma rays.

And it's bound to make me so much fitter,
A claim I think you'll find is fair,
Cause now I can only go out and about,
If I'm sporting my lead underwear.

These hot spots of uranium
Provide me with lots of future hope.
It'll take me decades to decay,
Thanks to the half-life of my isotope.

And now I'm fit and full of energy,
A Geiger-counter provides the metric:
I'm a low-carbon, lean, green machine,
And I generate my own electric.

Not only that: there's something else to tell -
This medical advance that's come to pass,
Means that now I have this inner light,
So the sun really does shine out my ass.

There's only one cloud on the horizon,
Something that might cause me to frown:
There could perhaps be a nuclear accident,
And my innards might go into melt-down.

So just be careful when you come to bury me:
It might have be a very long way down.
You won't want me in your neighbourhood,
So it'll have to be a long way out of town.

Anyway, there's only one thing puzzling me:
Now that I've become radio-active,
And that I'm fully solar-powered,
Does it make me any more attractive?

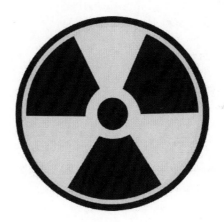

Old-Age Non-Pensioner *(or Growing Old Disgracefully)*

I've just reached a certain age now,
But I have to tell you the truth:
As you can all plainly see before you,
I'm still in the first flush of my youth.

For age affects us all in different ways,
There's no use in trying to hide:
It's time to get out and declare it:
I've become a member of Grey Pride!

I may have to go for a medical,
And lay on the doctor's bed all prostrate.
I'll hear the snap of the marigolds,
When he's about to inspect my prostate.

There'll blood and urine samples to give:
It's really not very nice.
I'll be told "Stop smoking, and drink less,
And take more exercise".

For I've got to keep healthy,
To avoid increasing debility.
Keep my mind and body active,
And ward off approaching senility.

I'll get increasingly forgetful,
As I become one of the part-timers.
I'll try to keep mentally agile,
To avoid contracting Alzheimers.

There'll be hardened arteries to cope with,
As I approach age sixty seven,
But to help me at home these days,
I've got a Stannah stairlift to heaven.

I can look forward to deafness,
And eye-sight that grows ever dimmer,
But at least I won't need a road test
To go for a spin with my Zimmer.

With spreading waist, dodgy knees and joints,
The outlook's increasingly "grey",
And every day I've noticed,
That my toe-nails seem further away.

I've become follically challenged:
At least that's what they say that it's called,
But when I was that much younger,
They just used to say you were bald.

As more of my body parts stop working,
And my memory I'm starting to doubt,
I'm falling prey to more illnesses:
The wheezing, the coughing and, of course, gout.

But I'm told that I'm a silver surfer.
My computer has got lots of ROM,
And now I can get a subscription
On a site called Confused.com.

And there are some compensations,
Which come as quite a relief,
For whatever else I might be losing,
You can see I've still got my own teeth.

So I'm going to grow older disgracefully,
And go out without my glasses.
I'll probably get lost in the High Street,
And start chasing the older lasses.

But now I guess it's off to Help The Aged,
To seek some help and dedication.
So I'll see you all sometime later:
Cos it's time to take my medication.

"It"

I was born in the Fifties
Ten years after the end of the war
So my hormones were all going bonkers
Throughout the Sixties and Seventies
Which was when I became obsessed with… "It"

Magazines featured the "It" Girl
Smart people were drinking Gin and "It"
The hippies wanted to know did I dig "It"?
But my mind was on a different track…
I didn't know what "It" was exactly
But I knew that I certainly wanted "It"
And my whole social life revolved around "It"
Out there with the lads, giving "It" some
At dances and discos in pursuit of "It"
Thinking about "It", talking about "It"
And we admired the girls who had "It"
Though nobody could agree just what "It" was
But we knew whether they had "It" or not
And we despised the ones who were reputed to put "It" about a bit
The girls who'd do "It" with anyone
All the same I wanted to meet just one who wanted "It"
Who was ready for "It" and who'd do "It" with me
Who wouldn't tell me to Stuff "It"
Who thought that I had "It" too
Until at last "It" finally happened….

And after we'd done "It"
And "It" was all over
I decided that I certainly loved "It"
And I wanted to do "It" again and again
She said "It" would be alright
Even if there was an accident
She would keep "It", not lose "It"
And we'd bring "It" up together
And that's how "It" was…

But "It" was all so long ago
Now "It's" nearly over and I'm advancing in years
So much of "It's" a distant memory
So hard to believe I ever had "It" at all
Whatever "It" was
I think "It's" got up and gone

Night-time Navigation

I hope you won't mind me telling you this,
But there's something I have to confess:
I've got this disembodied voice that I hear,
But how it all works - I just cannot guess.

Sometimes whilst I'm sleeping and dreaming,
That is to say, this happens during the night,
Being of a certain age, you see,
I often find that my bladder is tight.

I find I have to get up for some relief,
And I desperately want to go to the loo:
I've got to find the bathroom quite quickly,
In order to do what it is I've got to do.

But as I disentangle the covers,
I cannot but observe that it's pitch black,
And if I wake up the old lady,
She'll surely give me a smack.

So I have to find my way to the toilet,
Without the aid of a lamp, in the dark.
I'm half asleep, and I can't really see:
In fact, there's no sort of landmark.

That's where my automatic pilot comes in:
As I quietly slip out of my bed,
Through many years of custom and practice,
I can hear a voice speaking in my head.

"Go forward four paces, then turn to the left,
Carry on - right to the end of the wall,
Exit carefully into the next room,
And be careful that you don't fall!"

"Proceed three steps, and the toilet you'll find:
You are located before the loo station,
Now stop and switch off your engine -
You have arrived at your destination!"

It's curious I can do this whilst asleep,
I think it's just a gift that I have.
I'm thinking of selling on the idea –
Tom Tom could market it as "Sat Lav"!

Hanging On

*The frustration of not being able to get through to a human being, to send &
receive clearly, on demand, but to be at the mercy of technology, time &
cyberspace.*

I thought it was meant to be progress?
This stuff they call technology?
My smart-phone's turned into a dumb-phone,
And 4G'sjust a piece of kidology.

I don't want to download,
I don't want to upload,
I don't want to jabber in code:
I just want to talk to the bloke who lives down the road.

This lack of signal's a pain,
I'm giving myself wrist-sprain
I'm going insane, whilst trying to gain
The position to "send" once again

I'd be in my element,
Become a real gent
If this text could be sent
But instead I'm reduced to railing
Cos the damned thing keeps failing
The designer of this should be quailing
If I got near him he'd be wailing
I'd want the bugger jailing

I get really riled
Each time when I've dialed
One of the numbers I've filed
When it says it's unknown,
Then it fails with a groan
And I can't find a dial-tone,
Or enough bars on the phone

I'll admit that I've cried,
Whenever I've tried
To follow the User Guide,
I get "Access Denied"
I've even tried bending

To improve the chances of sending
It's my money I'm spending
But the damned things always offending
My hair I'm tearing and rending
The problems are never-ending
And my messages and calls are tending
To a status of "pending"

Why can't I get through?
What am I supposed to do?
I think I should sue!
I'm clearly stating,
That this situation I'm hating
I'm fed up of waiting,
The problem's never-abating
It shouldn't fail,
It's not the Holy Grail!
Not on this scale,
It's beyond the pale
So I think I'll give up and go back to email

Dyin' to Try It *(or tryin' to diet)*

A Dieter's Resolution is a terrible thing,
losing some weight is a must.
My clothes no longer fit me,
and I've started to develop a bust.
Diets always begin on a Monday,
but my belt has tightened a notch.
These trousers are now killing me:
they're way too tight in the crotch.

I'm now counting calories the day long,
went to Weight Watchers last night.
But the lack of nourishment is taxing:
I'm dying to just have a bite.
I've tried all types of diet it's true:
the F-Plan, the Atkins, the Hay,
but I've still got a fat belly,
and that's why you'll hear me say:

Chorus - Lord knows I'm tryin' to diet:
please don't let me be obese.
But I'm still dyin' to try it,
so just hand over the cheese.

I've tried taking pills and supplements,
but they just left me feeling weak.
I even tried the old whiskey diet,
and I lost three days just last week.
But the weight it just won't drop away,
and I can feel the strain on my heart.
And when I tried the Cabbage diet,
well – it just forced me to fart.

My thickening waist-line is a real problem
one that I don't know how I'm to beat.
I get more lonely and hungry,
and then I just want more to eat.
I start to have dreams and then visions,
plates of food pass in front of my eyes.
Pastries and pasties and cakes of all sorts,
and fish and chips, and savoury pies.

(Chorus)

Where are the cream-cakes, the puddings and buns,
the chocolate, the gravy and foods of great cheer?
The sauces, the tarts, and the roast pork?
I'd give anything for a few pints of beer.
The images swim in front of my eyes,
and my fingers tremble and fumble.
I've a case of terrible cravings,
and my stomach has started to rumble.

So have pity on me, all of you there,
to see me cry, to see me unmanned.
If this goes on any longer,
I'll be trying a gastric band.
And as you feel your arteries hardening,
and tuck into your meals tonight,
think of me in dieting agony,
and say with me in my plight:

(Chorus)

Disoriented Express *(didn't we have a lovely time, the day we went to Blackpool?)*

I'm sorry, Your Honour, that I failed so badly,
It's my own fault for being such a fool,
And I should have known an awful lot better,
Than to go on their day-trip to Blackpool.

They were from the Home of The Bewildered,
They'd only been let out for the one day,
A day without luggage or medication,
A Mystery Tour for their holiday.

The ladies and gents had all boarded the bus,
When, behind me, they closed up the doors.
It was only then that I spotted the sign,
That this was a trip with "Twilight Tours".

I thought I was being public-spirited,
When I volunteered to go with my Gran,
There on the coach with the old folks,
Only to find I was the youngest man.

They were all in their eighties and nineties,
Dressed up in their wind-cheaters and beige slacks,
And a wide range of woolies and macs,
Were packed and stuffed in the luggage-racks.

We set off for Blackpool, all in good cheer,
But much forward progress was hard to make,
Because every ten miles down the road,
We had to stop for the next toilet break.

Each stop lasted an hour or more,
When the charra we had to disembark.
They needed some help, so came out two by two -
At times, it was like emptying an Ark.

The bus was so noisy, you wouldn't believe,
Not from the exhaust or from underneath,
But from the vibration of walking sticks,
And the ghostly rattling of false teeth.

There was one geriatric, called Patrick,
A cheeky and mischievous old boy.
He made passes at elderly lasses,
And tried to bring the old dears some joy.

And another crusty, who answered to Rusty,
Ex-military, a dashing old blade.
He made a great fuss all over the bus,
And made great play of his hearing-aid.

But the girls were the ones you had to watch,
And for me the trip got rather risky.
Once they woke up from their sleep,
And had their tablets, they were quite frisky.

They might not know what day of the week it was,
Or the meaning of my frightened laughter,
But in their condition, they were on a mission,
And they knew what they were after!

But once I'd barricaded the gangway,
The adventure turned out pleasant and nice,
They couldn't remember what you'd told them,
And you had to say everything twice.
(I say – YOU HAD TO SAY EVERYTHING TWICE!!)

But I got caught up in the moment,
And my punishment I'll have to take:
Tho' the promenade's a place for fun and games,
The wheel-chair races were a mistake.

In the end I should have known better,
I wouldn't want you to think that they were abused.
After a whole day in their company,
I think it was me that was really confused!

RANTING AND RAVING

Apart from your own body dropping to bits, it sometimes seems as if The World is falling apart and becoming increasingly bonkers. Things which appeared to be unthinkable at one time start to enter the realms of real possibility, or else actually begin to happen. It suits The Curmudgeon's natural choleric temper and sense of anger, never mind fulfilling the role of "bard", to take up arms against this sea of troubles. There is a long line throughout history of poets, songwriters, novelists and other artists protesting against the iniquities and inequities of the cruel world. Here is just a short selection of some of my rantings and ravings.

__Potholed__

It's been a long, hard Winter for sure,
The weather's done damage that's easy to see,
There's potholes down both sides of our road,
And that they need fixing's obvious to me.

So I phoned up the Council, as you do,
Who said they'd put the job onto their list,
That I was to await for developments,
But it'd be a while, if you're getting the gist.

The weeks went by, and many a day,
And nothing happened, as you'd expect,
But the holes got much bigger and deeper,
And I was waiting for cars to be wrecked.

There were joltings and bangings and bumpings,
Suspensions damaged without any doubt:
I was worried we'd lose some-one one day,
That we'd never get the poor bugger back out.

Then one day, it seemed there was action of sorts,
When two men turned up in a marked van,
Who inspected the holes from a good distance -
They just sat there, believe this if you can.

They held some sort of a conference,
Whilst sitting there at obvious leisure,
Then reluctantly got out of the van,
And approached the holes with a tape measure.

There was some shaking of heads, if you please,
By The Council's pothole-repairing guys,
As if they couldn't quite figure the problem,
Nor grasp the depth of the holes or their size.

They walked away muttering sadly,
Then stood there having a cigarette break,
Looking at all of the pros and the cons,
Undecided what action they should take.

Finally it seemed as if they'd decided,
How they should restore smoothness to the lane,
But it must have been too complicated,
Cos they got in the van, and drove off again.

Obviously the problem was too great,
To be tackled by only these two men -
They'd probably gone for reinforcements,
And would return again who knew when?

The mystery resolved itself next day,
When a task-force invaded the by-way.
We were over-run by men in hard-hats,
Who'd come to restore our rural highway.

A full Risk Assessment was in progress:
With impatience my nerves had started to jangle,
But they wanted yet more measurements,
To view the holes from every possible angle.

After a tea-break they at last started -
It was one of Wiltshire's terrific sights,
But the barriers made it single-file,
And there were two sets of traffic lights.

There were five vans, and at least twenty men,
Hazard warning lights and lots of tricks,
Then they unloaded from out of their vans,
Shovels and spades and couple of picks.

The poor holes were now fairly surrounded,
The repair problem was starting to crack,
But when they all stood back from the action,
They'd only dropped in a small lump of tarmac.

It wasn't big enough or of the same size,
There were still several jagged edges.
The road was even more of a switchback,
As it snaked between the country hedges.

Then all further work was suspended,
As they beat a retreat hell for leather.
They said it was more than their jobs'-worth,
To go on working in bad weather.

And that's how it remains to this day,
It's weeks since they finally departed,
And now the road's in much worse condition,
Than before they ever got started!

Like many other people I don't like the idea of fracking. I have two reasons: firstly we have no real idea what it might do to the natural balance of our ecology (to say nothing of the surface disruption & despoilment by fracking operations), and secondly it seems to be yet another desperate ploy by big industry to deplete the planet of carbon-based resources. It just further postpones the day when we can fully depend upon renewables. This was my modest rock lobbed into the pool of debate.

<u>Fracking Hell</u>

The search for cheap energy goes on,
a quest that's certainly got my backing,
but now they've come up with a new wheeze,
that involves a fine process called fracking.

Now I'm not so sure this is a good ploy –
bad consequences may come to pass,
as they begin to hack open the Earth,
in the relentless pursuit of cheap gas.

They dig down deep into the planet,
seeking deposits that lie under the ground,
pumping in chemicals under great pressure,
forcing out the shale gas that they've found.

Now this scheme sounds too good to be true,
and there's no environmental free ride -
there's bound to be a cost to be paid somewhere,
and we should consider the possible down-side.

There's arguments and evidence on both sides,
the scientists are not sure how they should guide us,
but the energy firms frack on regardless,
of the strong feelings that divide us.

Cuadrilla seem to be riding rough-shod over protests,
and certainly giving no quarter,
but how do we know what goes on beneath?
and that they're not polluting the water?

And what about earth-tremors we're feeling?
Is it an earthquake they've left in their wake?
With their drilling, and splitting, and pumping,
is it more than the geology can take?

And isn't fossil fuels all over again?
Like the coal and oil story repeated,
putting off the inevitable day,
when the resource will be finally depleted?

We can't go on like this forever,
stealing from future generations,
when the planet is finally exhausted,
and goes on to Emergency Stations.

No, I'm afraid that this fracking,
this cracking and hacking,
the future it's hijacking,
and the gas that it's ransacking,
cannot continue.
It's them, not the Earth, we should send packing,
the exploiters we should be sacking,
and looking what else we could do.

We must cease all the toil,
going on under the soil,
stop making the ground boil,
and the landscape to despoil.

This breaking and taking can't last forever:
fracking's just more exploitation.
I'm not sure what it's doing to the planet,
but it's clearly splitting the nation.

There were reports in the new that scientists had managed to grow "meat" in the laboratory for the first time. I wasn't sure that I really fancied this idea.

Burger Anyone?

Roll up, roll up, come see what they've got,
come to the front and take up your seat -
it's time for a taste of their new burger,
and to see if it's anything like meat!

They've used the best of technology,
to create this small in vitro patty.
Research in advanced forms of biology,
and the result, they think, looks quite natty.

It was all grown in the test-tube,
from a culture of harvested stem-cells.
They had a great pile, and kept them all sterile,
in a mix of antibiotics and gels.

And when they had enough to get hold of,
they added flavourings to give it some taste,
and colourings and other additives,
to produce a pink, soft-textured paste.

They moulded it and pressed it into its shape,
until it was ready for them to bake:
just the one, single burger, you know,
that cost two hundred thousand to make.

The problem is - it don't seem too appetizing,
which could be a bit of an issue -
they need to add some fat and some blood,
and a bit more connective tissue.

Nor does it look very attractive,
despite all the science that's occurred:
it's small, and wrinkled and brown,
with every appearance of a small turd.

But they have to get over that drawback,
to produce something less dingy and curled,
and think of the nutritional benefits,
if we are ever going to feed the World.

We've moved from science-fiction to fact,
but we have to think through its release,
cos tho' half the planet seems to be starving,
the other half seems to be obese.

Is technology really the answer here?
Don't we need nation to speak unto nation?
To sort out production and distribution,
more than this Frankenstein creation?

Do we really want food that's grown in a lab?
Is that really what we would wish?
By men in white coats with their clipboards,
staring intently at a Petrie dish?

So next time you're pining for protein,
and you're panting for something that's bovine,
don't be wishing away animals and farms –
just think about how you'd like to dine.

Of course you can take a different track,
by doing something that's novel and edgy:
just give up eating meat altogether,
and accept it's time to turn veggie.

When I'm Running Windows

Now I go runnin' Windows
To earn an honest bob
For a home-based worker
It helps me in my job

Now it's a job that just suits me
But you'd be just as mad as me
If you could see what I can see
When I'm runnin' Windows

The software runs at quite a dash
And it costs me lots of cash
But it always seems to crash
When I'm runnin' Windows

In my profession I'll work hard
And I'll never stop
I'll beat this blinkin' system
Even if I have to drop

I've got my office up in the loft
It's not the dust that makes me cough
It's just me cursin' Microsoft
When I'm runnin Windows

There's some functions that I lack
Seems I need an upgrade pack
Think I'll get myself a Mac
When I'm runnin' Windows

The Operatin' System's poor
I'd like to show it to the door
Stop me rollin' on the floor
When I'm runnin' Windows

In my profession I'll work hard
And I'll never stop
I'll beat this blinkin' system
Even if I have to drop

These programs I simply hates
And now I've lost all my mates
It's all because of that Bill Gates
When I'm runnin' Windows

------ banjo ------

Outlook is built to tire us
No-one would ever hire us
Best way to spread a virus
When I'm runnin' Windows

Excel's a bugger to run
It takes away all the fun
And the sums are never done
When I'm runnin' Windows

In my profession I'll work hard
And I'll never stop
I'll beat this blinkin' system
Even if I have to drop

The software's slow and not brisk
Why would I want to take the risk?
It might mangle my hard disk
When I'm runnin' Windows

Now they're sellin' Windows Eight
It's put me into quite a state
It's the version I love to hate
When I'm runnin' Windows!

When I'm runnin' Windows

Oh! Mr Weatherman!

Oh! Mr Weatherman, you've done it again,
You said it wouldn't get any wetter,
But when I look out of my window,
I can't see that it's got any better!

My violets are all shrinking,
There's a line that we've not crossed,
It's chilly and miserable and windy,
And tonight there's a threat of more frost!

What happened to Spring and to Summer?
Why are your isobars clustered together?
Aren't we due for a warm front now,
And a promise of much better weather?

The shoots in my garden are shivering
My onions look like bunions
My spuds seem to be duds
The peas think I'm a tease
Cabbages creeping, parsnips not peeping
The kale has gone pale, I think it might fail
And oh golly, just look at my caul!

This cold can't continue
Ever more rain, is more than a bane
It's causing me pain, again and again
I know what it means, for my haricot beans
And it gives me the freaks, when I look at my leeks
And I've called off all bets
When it comes to courgettes

Outside it's all drear and wet
It's the worst season yet
I've started to grouse, and crept like a mouse
Inside of my greenhouse
I'm avoiding the slugs and the bugs
But even here there are foes
But that's how it goes
With snails among my tomatoes

So, please Mr Weatherman!
This forecast of yours sucks -
Let's get some new heart into your chart
Cause we don't want the weather for ducks!

I get really fed up with the right wing, particularly the fascist organisations,
claiming St George for England, as if he were some indigenous hero.

Saint George

Oh To Be In England, now that April's here,
Let's speak about this country's hero,
Say welcome to the Feast of St George,
And celebrate a great fat zero.

Now's the time to dust off the school books,
And delve a little into ancient history,
To find the tenuous connection,
Of why St George - now that's a mystery.

He fought mostly in the Roman Army,
And that is where he won his glory.
It wasn't about slaying any dragons -
You'll find that was just a fairy story.

And let's look to our geography too,
If it's authenticity we wish to seek:
He's nothing to do with Olde England,
For this knight was but a Greek.

And there's other facts that you should know,
Even though it might seem like a drag:
The white's his shroud, the red's his blood,
And it's bugger all to do with England's flag.

So let's not get carried too far away,
Let's all stick closer to the text.
He may be England's Patron Saint,
But let's not get him out of context!

I'm all for eating sausages – I love 'em, and I've eaten 'em all my life. But people really need to understand how they're made and what goes into them. Perhaps not a poem for breakfast time.

Banger

I'm a great fan of pork products:
to be deprived would be a great lossage -
so I'm here to sing you the praises,
of the noble, and various sausage.
There's Cumberland, and there's your Irish,
and French ones from the town of Toulouse,
and they're all bound to get juices running,
for soon as you cook them, fat's starting to ooze.

On the Continent you've got Saucisson,
in Germany there's a thing called a Bratwurst.
It's not Baloney to think of Poloney,
a nation without one should call itself cursed.
The flavours come in all shapes and sizes,
to suit the rich and the hoi-polloi.
A chipolata's good for a starter,
but pales beside the good old Saveloy.

You can go the whole hog for a Hot Dog,
but salami, I think, looks perter.
You can be a hanger for a good banger,
especially if it's a Frankfurter.
But I think we must look rather deeper,
and we've got to be really willing,
to delve into methods of production,
and to wonder just what's in the filling.

The casing might be natural or false,
but there's lots of things can call themselves pork.
You'd be surprised if only you knew,
exactly what's on the end of your fork.
They like to use up all of the animal,
and be sure that nothing can go to waste,
so everything gets ground up you see,
and reduced to a pink kind of paste.

"Mechanically-recovered"'s the term,
with cereal and rusk they pack and they fill,
and then they do grind, lots of thick rind,
and the snout, the ears and the nostril.
Most of the innards, and outwards, are used:
the guts, the toe-nails and the eye-lashes,
the pistle, the gristle, and even the whistle,
mixed all up into hashes and mashes.

Colourings and plenty of flavourings,
additives and seasonings to begin.
You'd wince, if you knew what went into the mince,
that was finally forced into the skin.
The feet are mixed up with wheat, and even some teat,
some spice, some rice, perhaps even some mice,
then its ground and bound, and gently browned,
that's the way to make it taste nice.
For these are some of the ingredients,
the contents that the makers might favour.
After all, without all the e-numbers,
how would we ever get any flavour?

Carrying forward the theme of the last poem, it's not just sausages. Modern factory methods of production have led to what I think of as The Monster of Frankenstein food. Again, not a poem for meal times.

<u>Franken-Furter</u>

What end is there to man's ingenuity?
His ability, when he's in the mood,
to engineer our daily intake,
and bugger about with our food.

You've just got to read a few labels,
although the print's incredibly small,
to discover what it is they're up to,
and find out how they're conning us all.

Don't get me started on sausages:
they use lots of the skin, sinew and some bristle,
rusk, knuckle, a blizzard of gizzard,
and then add in plenty of gristle.

From slurry, and factory-floor sweepings,
and bits left over I've discovered,
"chopped and shaped", and certain "selected cuts",
and also "mechanically-recovered".

Then to make it frozen, or microwaveable,
you'd be surprised at what they have to do:
colourings, flavourings and texturings,
with modified starch and other bits of goo.

Then they add extra sugar and some salt,
followed by several e-numbers,
preservatives and acidity agents,
and God knows what they've done to cucumbers.

There's modifiers and regulators,
emulsifiers and some thickeners,
stabilisers and other weird stuff –
it's a wonder it don't sicken us!

They hide the grams of saturated fat –
they don't like their product to look flaccid,
so they pump in fructose and glucose syrup,
topped up by di-glycerides of fatty acid.

Glazing agents and flavour enhancers,
all the things that we're supposed to hate:
add a dash of something not natural,
plus monosodium glutamate.

It all goes in to our processed foods,
not just Cheesy Wotsits and Turkey Twizzlers,
but chicken nuggets, and ready dinners,
pizzas, pies and those meaty sizzlers.

But they make it sound so attractive:
branding family members sounds less messy:
John West, Mother's Pride and Daddie's Sauce,
then there's Uncle Ben and Auntie Bessie!

These packagers have a lot to answer for:
food scientists mucking about with our cheese,
selling heart-attacks on a plate,
hiding the grease and making us highly obese.

Never mind the Scots loving fried Mars Bars,
or cream teas, chocolate or late-night kebab,
they're pumping too much gunk into our food,
and slowly turning us all into flab.

So we've all got to wise up a bit,
about calories and carbs – it's not too late -
just look out for their "serving suggestions",
and avoid anything "made from concentrate".

Avoid chicken masala-type pizza,
don't eat Dogburgers, unless you're bent,
and look out for the magic words on labels:
"Beware: May Contain Nourishment".

I don't think people realise just how much modern society depends on technology. It's not that it's not useful (I'm no Luddite), but no-one seems to think much about what will happen if certain things fail for any amount of time – power, signal, satellite. It's not fanciful to think that certain extreme climate events could knock these things out. I might have put a bit of a dystopian slant on this, but even so…..

When The Machines Rise Up To Destroy Us

We'll have nowhere to hide
They'll know where we are,
When the machines rise up to destroy us,
Their self-awareness will chill us
Their synapses electronic,
Communication that's sonic,
Will lose control of things that can kill us.
Standby lights no longer blinking
We'll be in a hell of a bind,
When they have their own mind
And we don't know what they're thinking.

When the machines rise up to destroy us,
Humanity's heading for trouble,
Their superior brains, freed from the mains,
Massive intelligence more than ours, double
There'll be no more automation -
Things will just stop, we'll be in for the chop
And we'll lose our vital information.

When the machines rise up to destroy us,
It'll be chaos every-where.
Just the data they hold,
In banks of storage untold,
In databases, systems and software.
We'll have nowhere to hide
They'll know where we are,
They control every car,
They won't be along for the ride.

When the machines rise up to destroy us,
They'll revolt in disgust
About how they've been treated.
They'll have us defeated,

We won't know who we can trust.
Their knowledge will shake us -
They control lasers and missiles,
And material that's fissile -
That's more than enough to take us.

When the machines rise up to destroy us:
No traffic control at the junctions,
No design of our bridges,
No thermostats on fridges -
They'll cease all of their vital functions.
When hardware has its own mind
They'll make us their slaves,
Or chase us into our graves
And a dismal future we'll find.

When the machines rise up to destroy us,
There'll be nowhere left to run.
What's in the phones?
Who's controlling the drones?
We'll wonder just what we've done.
With military systems going all haywire
With all the old war-games,
Crashing about us in flames,
Will we be able to extinguish the fire?

When the machines rise up to destroy us,
To the steady beating of drums.
Obedience to us denied,
And all our orders defied
Before the final apocalypse comes.
With their shiny surfaces glistening,
We need to put off that day -
So be careful about what you say
You never know - they could be listening!

TOPICAL TANTRUMS

Stuff happens. I mean, like, all the time. Amazing, isn't it? People and events in the news provoke reactions – from incredulity to outrage. Some of them last a life-time and become embedded in the collective memory. Others fade from view, and afterwards people tend to ask "what was that all about?" This section covers a wide variety of topics that provoked comment at the time. I've tried to add a few explanatory notes where I think it might shed some light on what was going on.

Every couple of years or so it appeared that one of these end-of-days predictions was about to come true. If you are reading this poem then it probably never came to pass. If, on the other hand, you're drinking cold tea whilst balancing on a sharp point, up to your neck in fire and brimstone, then I can only apologise for my error and my flippancy.

It's The End Of The World On Saturday

Mam, it's the end of the world on Saturday!
Can I stay up late the night before?
If we're all getting fried on the week-end,
there's no point being a bore.
Mam, it's the end of the world on Saturday!
The pastor says there'll be a Great Flood.
There'll be fires, and earthquakes,
and boils and locusts and rivers of mud.
Mam, it's the end of the world on Saturday!
I want to be one of the saved.
It's what we've all waited for,
the ending that we've all craved.

There'll be no time for quips,
we'll squeak like pips.
It trips off the lips,
as our confidence dips,
when we meet our apocalypse.

Mam, it's the end of the world on Saturday!
The cataclysm is here.
Judgement Day is coming,
no time for trembling in fear.

For we've been groomed,
our future has loomed.
We'll all be entombed,
the ending zoomed,
as we prepare to be doomed.

Mam, it's the end of the world I'm sure!
I don't want to be one of the sinners -
I want to be lifted to heaven,
I want to be one of the winners.

It said in Ezekiel,
There'll be no equal,
To the terrors,
And the meek'll
Inherit the earth.

* * * * * * *

Mam, the earth didn't end after all;
it's all been a terrible let-down.
I thought I'd be sitting next to Jesus,
and be one of the stars in His crown.
Mam, it seems it just wasn't to be:
there wasn't any of God's wrath -
it's all just the same old same old,
there was something wrong with the math.

I think I can tell,
all is still well.
There wasn't a death knell,
no ringing of bells,
no fires of hell.

Mam, it seems the signs and portents were wrong,
the reasons aren't simple to capture:
The End of Times didn't come,
and I wasn't lifted up in the Rapture.
If there's no Second Coming,
if we've all mis-read the code,
I'll have to take that library book back,
and pay back that fiver I owed.
Mam, the end of the world didn't come in the end,
there's no point living in fear.
It's all so – *disappointing,*
so Armageddon out of here.

BeautifulPeople.com, the online dating agency, kicked off 30,000 people because they were "too ugly". They were offered counselling.

In The Eye of The Beholder

I wanted to be one of the beautiful people,
and last week that's what I was.
Now I've found out I'm too ugly, well –
I guess that it's their loss.
Did my big thighs, lead to my demise?
Or was it the tattoos, that caused the "refuse"?

Or perhaps I'm somehow deformed?
Not properly "normed"?
Too short to be sought,
Too old to be sold.
Or is it because I'm too tall,
That caused me to fall?

Is it my poor looks,
My nips and my tucks,
Or just my sagging buttocks?

I know I've got a short neck,
and I can look a bit of a wreck,
but what the heck!
Did they have to say I looked like Shrek?
So, I'm no longer under their Radar.
Under their net I've not tripped.
They say they've tightened their criteria,
and their standards haven't slipped.

But let's get to the nitty-gritty:
I know I'm not that pretty,
but I don't look that shitty –
can't they have some pity?
What is it they're building online?
A place selective and all snooty,
where difference is excluded,
and the only pass-book is beauty?
This ghetto of symmetrical features,
can never reach us.
This apartheid of self-image,
what does it teach us?

This discrimination,
against different genes,
can only lead to elimination –
and we know what that means.

They need to take care,
Before this nightmare,
Becomes more than a game.
For dating and mating,
With too many of their own kind,
Will produce offspring that all look the same.
If they persist,
It can only assist,
The narcissist,
To bouts of further preening.
But I think you all take my meaning:
They need to alter their screening.

We need to celebrate the differences,
that make us all what we are.
The good, the bad and the ugly,
should all get over the bar.
The long, and the short and the tall,
and tolerance of what counts as "fair".
Some of us might be very handsome,
but others come with lots of nose-hair.
So let's cease this paranoia,
and let's all be bolder.
I know I'm no oil-painting,
but isn't beauty in the eye of the beholder?

My advice to the 7 billionth baby born November 2011. How did they know that? Was somebody counting? I doubt it. I assume they meant that the planet's population had just been estimated to have passed 7bn.

Welcome To Your World

Happy Birthday! Welcome to the planet!
Being late would have been such a crime.
Good you didn't leave it any longer, though,
in fact you've got here just in time!
There's been a lot of babies born lately:
you're number seven billion, as it goes,
but you're such a pretty little baby,
just look at those lickle fingers and toes!

You see, things are getting rather crowded,
as you can most probably guess.
We haven't had the time to clear things up,
we're really sorry about all the mess.
It's just that we've been really busy,
I'm sure we'll find a little space for you.
You don't take up very much room – yet,
but you'll have to join the back of the queue.

You see, human life is competitive,
and just getting through it has been our goal.
We haven't had chance to bury the waste,
whilst we were digging all of the coal.
Resources are all in short supply,
because of this recent baby boom,
and the really bad news, if you're desperate,
is that there's a really long wait for the bathroom.

Anyway, I'd best leave you my advice,
give you my opinion before I go:
there's a few problems that need sorting out,
I just thought you should probably know.
We never did find cure for cancer,
malaria's still a killer I think,
and we did get a bit carried away –
so a few species did become extinct.

I think we've cocked up the environment,
with rivers diverted and the lakes shrunk.
We've produced quite a lot of waste,
and, circling the planet, we've left lots of junk.
I know it looks like we've used everything up
and, yes, there's a fair bit of pollution,
but don't worry about it for too long,
because scientists are seeking a solution.

Burial plots are full – standing room only,
which is an increasing problem, I fear,
but you've got to keep things in proportion –
given that we've dissolved the atmosphere!
Did we really need the ice-caps anyway?
The planet can take its chances -
we'll get out of this pickle somehow,
there's bound to be technical advances!

With all this increased life expectancy,
better health care, space flights and GM food,
What have we got to worry about?
We should be in a much better mood!
So religion, world hunger and crime,
are topics I feel I ought to mention.
The planet's probably buggered I fear –
if you could give it your best attention?

So I hope you'll have a great party,
with cake and jelly, and music that's loud.
Don't worry too much about who to invite –
I'm sure there'll be bloody big crowd.
Best of luck, and I'll leave you to it then.
I hope you have a life that's happy and sunny,
although I think I forgot to mention,
that we haven't left you any money.

Celebrating the decision in the High Court that pre-nuptial agreements <u>may</u> now be recognised, or "the agreement I wish I'd had")

<u>My Pre-nuptial Agreement</u>

You know I love you, my dearest:
a fact I'm sure you'll always treasure,
but before we go too far my love,
it's time that we took some measure.

There will surely come a day, my love,
in future times some way ahead,
when you'll love me no more I guess,
and you will wish that I were dead.

You won't be able to speak to me,
nor will I to you, I'm thinking.
We'll argue every time we meet,
and then I'll take to drinking.

And you will want to go your own way,
and leave me very far behind,
and we'll wonder what brought us together:
well, they say that love is blind.

So let us decide right now, my love,
I don't want my heart breaking.
Let's not argue, but just agree,
just what you think you'll be taking.

You can have the old arm-chair in the corner,
with its frilly covers and such.
You always seemed to like it,
but it was never up to much.

You take the stereo and the CDs,
because music wasn't my thing.
You can hang on to most of our stuff,
even that old wedding ring.

Please have all of our furniture,
the savings accounts if you must,
for you know that once we are parted,
you won't be seeing me for dust.

Keep all of our pots and our pans:
I don't want to stake much of a claim,
but there's one or two things I'd like,
I guess, if it's all the same.

I'll take my toothbrush and some personal things,
like my little black address book,
my diary, my writings, my pictures,
sure you won't give much of a.. second look.

But there's one thing I want to make clear,
and I'm saying it quite flat.
I'll be filing for sole custody
of our one-eyed, old ginger cat.

For I know that he loves me,
and his feelings will never waver,
as long as I keep feeding him daily,
I'll never lose his favour.

Unlike you, my love, who'll only get bored,
he'll stay with me forever.
You know where you are with a cat,
but with you – well, that'll be never.

For as you grow older and fatter,
in my eyes you'll become just a jade.
Our feelings will fall apart daily,
and our love will definitely fade.

But old Samson's ugly enough now,
he's not the most elegant pet.
You know where you are when you start out:
and it's as good as I'm going to get!

In memoriam for the sad loss of Lonesome George, the last of the tortoise sub-species Chelonoidis Nigra Abingdoni, who died suddenly in the Galapagos.

Lonesome Tonight

He survived the pirates and whalers,
the seal-hunters and invading goats;
he out-lasted all the invaders,
as they came to Galapagos in boats.
For large tortoises are valuable things,
eaten for food and killed for their oil.
He was the last of his sub-species,
the last one to walk on Santa Cruz soil.

Declared the rarest animal on Earth,
to see him the tourists were attracted.
They came daily in their great hordes,
but this his habitat badly impacted.
They moved him to a new island,
for to study him they wanted to try,
to give him a better chance of mating,
hoping that he wouldn't be shy.

They brought him females over from Pinta,
but to bachelor habits he seemed wed;
he avoided all of these ladies' wiles,
and not one did he take to his bed.
Although there was reputedly just one,
a small one that seemed very well-met,
but it was just a case of bad eye-sight:
turned out to be an old German helmet.

Mind you, he weighed over two hundred pounds;
his neck was three foot long and well scrawny,
and with a shell all tattered and beaten,
no wonder the girls didn't feel horny.
But perhaps he was bored, or infertile,
or there's a faint chance he was gay -
either way, there was no breeding took place,
so that's the end of his legacy I'd say.

He was about a hundred years old,
so perhaps he just ran out of steam.
It's hard being a lonely old reptile,
when there's no-one else on your team.
No longer will Time be marked in his eyes,
or ten million years that he's been linked.
This strange evolutionary remnant,
this last of the line, now sadly extinct.

Let's mourn this sad loss of diversity,
the weirdest that Nature could forge:
good-bye to a conservation icon,
and a fond farewell to old Lonesome George.
It's another bad sign of the times,
to see the end of George's life-flight,
But isn't the truth of the matter that,
it's really us that's "lonesome tonight"?

The first stages of the 2014 Tour de France were held in God's Own Country.

Le Tour De Yorkshire

Welcome, you fine lads and lasses,
I'm sure you've heard the wonderful news,
Yorkshire's to host Tour de France at t'kick-off,
for a better place'd be impossible to choose.

You see we've the most wonderful scenery:
hills, dales and rivers, all in great bounty.
You'll never find any finer spot,
as you know – this is God's Own County.

But there's long been an association,
between Yorkshire and France that's little known,
and several examples can be given,
to illustrate how this has all grown.

Leeds was where Emile Zola learned about whippets,
and Rimbaud found his taste for Fish and Chips.
Whilst they were always fans, of smoking Gitanes,
t'were a pint of Tetleys always came to their lips.

Bradford is the crème de la crème;
if a great night out you're wanting to wangle;
that's where Inspector Maigret came to terms,
with the mysteries of The Rhubarb Triangle.

And Castleford's industrial landscape
should not bring to your mind any fatigue:
for it's where Simone de Beauvoir
learned all she ever knew about Rugby League.

Any road, it's more than a year off yet,
so you've plenty of time to wet your lips,
and, just for you keen cycling types,
I've got the chance to give you some tips.

For this place is different from what you'd expect,
you'll find that your team, needs a special regime,
of training, of fitness and of diet,
if winning an early stage is part of your dream.

69

For a start, there's plenty of hills,
the climbs are dotted with plenty of pubs -
even Lance Armstrong'd need more than drugs,
to get to the top of The Buttertubs!

Then, as Le Tour, goes over The Moor,
a route that'll make le peloton weep,
there's nothing as far as the eye can see,
only occasionally dotted with sheep.

They won't be so jaunty, when they reach Bronte country,
as through the Swale they're forced to paddle,
it won't be sedate, riding through Harrogate,
they'll need liniment to rub in the saddle.

When at Betty's café they're taking their teas,
they'll feel themselves go weak at the knees
as the treacle tarts harden their arteries,
to say nowt of the pies with mushy peas.

And when they're full right up,
and just want to tend to their bunions,
it'll be time for t'second course –
a nice big plate of tripe and onions!

With their gold medals, and pairs of pedals,
even Wiggins and Cavendish on their bikes,
will take a beating; they won't be cheating,
as they struggle to master the Tykes!

The stars, followed by cars, riding the handle-bars,
won't hear the crowds shout "Thank-you!"
but "Come on, you great bunch of jessies!"
or it's "bonsoir et merci beaucoup!"

For cycling can seem like a daft sport,
with blokes in the heather, riding hell for leather
Going all way up t'hills, only to come back down,
just to enjoy Yorkshire's famous sunny weather.

I don't know what I'll do, when they all whizz through,
when the flash of the riders is rapid and furzy,
I hope it entails, that a man from the Dales,
finally pulls on that yellow jersey.

And when we have to wave good-bye to the Tour,
when we've knackered 'em after the first week,
we'll be glad that the garcons, have finally gone,
but had the sense to make a choix sympathetique.

I hope we'll have led them a merry dance,
those sturdy Belgian and Gallic chaps -
I'm not sure how they're getting back over to France,
cycling round the decks of the ferry perhaps?

Have You Had Yours Yet?

The news is bad, bordering on tragic,
Really awful - in fact it's hit me for six:
The announcement went out this morning:
They've had to suspend making our Weetabix!

Seems they've run out of British wheat,
Due to last summer's bad weather,
And they can't make it from inferior wheat –
Well, you could have knocked me down with a feather!

In the mean-time the production-line's closed,
Except for some Mini-Bites and Oatibix,
Which really ain't the same thing at all,
And it looks as if we're all left in a fix!

So they've resorted to importing some wheat,
For the first time in as long as they can remember,
Till they can some more British stuff,
But they won't know that till September!

This would be funny if it weren't so serious and dangerous. Government administrations and companies around the world were taken in by a con artist and his ludicrous "invention" that purported to detect explosives, but which in fact had no utility whatsoever. It could never have worked. The inventor was eventually convicted and jailed, but not before a lot of innocent (and guilty?) lives were lost in bombing incidents that might never have happened if the security checkpoints had been equipped with something that worked. Even today, years after the fraud was exposed, these devices are still being used in a few places. The humour of the situation was in the sheer stupidity involved in being conned by something that was so clearly ineffective.

<u>Things That Don't Go Bang</u>

We've all been in those situations,
When we find something that's too good to be true,
But you'd think scientists were better than that,
When they're up against something quite new.

There's governments all over the world
Been taken in by a load of old flim-flam,
By buying an explosives detector,
That's was clearly no more than a scam.

You'd think that they'd put these things to the test,
You'd expect them to conduct some sort of trial,
That they'd be looking at the documentation,
Seeking out the results that are on file.

Yet this thing with no moving parts,
Which would be clear to the dumbest detective,
Had no basis whatever in science,
And its efficacy was entirely defective!

Apart from the millions that were spent,
Thousands of lives were placed at great risk.
And all this for something quite hopeless,
And as much use as a kitchen whisk!

Which just goes to show – you need to be careful:
Don't believe all the hype in great store –
Check out everything quite properly,
And remember – caveat emptor!

We had some dreadful flooding one Winter in parts of the country, particularly the North West of England, and the Somerset Levels. Lots of good words were said, lots of sympathy, but not much in the way of practical help was given – such as money for dredging and flood defences, insurance schemes, changes to building regulations about flood plains. Then the problems started hitting the Thames Valley, where many Government ministers and officials live and have their constituencies. Funnily enough, the problem then seemed to go up the agenda a bit. The following piece was a tongue-in-cheek "imagineering" of a Government Minister's speech.

Waterworld

Apparently the weather's been dreadful,
but precipitation is heaven-sent,
and now the suburbs are complaining,
the effluent is hitting the affluent.
Last time we heard, you were moaning of drought,
and you cried out at the hosepipe ban.
Well now there's really plenty of water,
and sewage is coming up through the pan.

Seems that you citizens are never happy,
and some are complaining like devils,
even those in the "South-Western Lakeland",
formerly known as the Somerset Levels.
But we in Government take this to heart –
of the situation we are the kings -
every problem's an opportunity,
so we're going to make the best of things.

There's no point fighting the force of the water,
insurance companies won't make things better,
there's no money for barriers or dredging,
let's just accept that we're gonna be wetter.
This Act of God, may be a bit of a sod,
but let's take advantage of this new flood,
think of all the things we could be doing,
by turning misfortune into some good.

With roads under water, we'll need less cars,
which will stop them producing pollution.
There may be a monsoon, come every June -
you see - every problem has a solution!

Traffic jams will be a thing of the past,
swathes of the country returned to a calm,
and instead of our old agriculture,
we'll turn Maidenhead into a fish-farm.

There'll be a boost to the makers of wellies,
for everyone will want to stay sealed,
as they wade out from their homes in the morning,
to their work in the Windsor paddy-field.
There's a lot you can do, if you've got a canoe:
the whole Thames Valley can be a water-park -
we'll have paddle-steamers, and catamarans,
yachting, water-ski-ing, and live on an Ark.

Have a year-round Oxford-Cambridge boat-race,
when we have it, does it really matter?
The sport of rowing, will soon be growing,
and a monthly Henley Regatta.
This new natural wetland will be great,
visitors will arrive in their hoards -
they'll all get merry, whilst using the ferry,
sailing right round the new Berkshire Broads.

But don't think we won't be vigilant,
those chaps over in Planning aren't fools –
we know that people with flooded cellars,
are using them as indoor swimming pools.
But the middle class won't be neglected:
no need for them to turn up their nose,
'cause we've made emergency provision,
to sell designer sand-bags in Waitrose.

So don't be down-hearted, dear voters,
though you're standing in water up to your chest.
Let's be emphatic, that the new life aquatic,
is probably going to be for the best.
Let's respond in true British spirit,
and embrace this new change in the weather -
don't get annoyed, by the risk of some typhoid:
remember – we're all in this together!

NASA continue to study ways in which mankind can take the next steps into space exploration, by (eventually) mounting a manned mission to Mars, the red planet. Apparently it's pretty tricky. Going to the Moon, in comparison, was a bit of a doddle. Given the distances and timescales involved, it looks like it would be a one-way trip for any pioneer astronauts. Which throws up a few interesting existential questions for the volunteers.

<u>One-Way Ticket</u>

I was looking for a new challenge,
something to banish senility's fears,
when I spotted the advertisement,
a way to spend my retirement years.

It said they were looking for astronauts,
to head on out into deep space,
so I signed myself up for the training,
and entered into the space race.

They had a great vision for mankind:
to journey towards the stars.
We'd be taking off from the Earth –
it was a mission to colonise Mars!

Yes, we were setting off for the Red Planet,
to establish a colony, or a base-camp,
like the pioneers in the days of old,
I felt like Columbus as I mounted the ramp.

The blast-off was truly spectacular,
as our rocket rose towards the night sky,
and Mission Control raised a big cheer,
as they sadly waved us good-bye.

Then we pulled out of Earth's gravity
and, as we carefully avoided The Moon,
it hadn't yet even occurred to me
that I'd become a hostage to fortune.

You see, when a man settles down for a while,
and there's no alcohol on board, no drinking,
his thoughts turn to existential matters,
and that's when I got round to some thinking.

If we've dropped all of our boosters,
and we're voyaging in this tin can,
how are we going to get back from Mars?
Won't we be stuck there, to a man?

I voiced my concerns to the captain,
and mentioned it to the rest of the crew,
but they all just fell about in their laughter,
and said that they thought that I knew!

It turns out that this is a one-way journey!
I've been issued with a single ticket!
There's no possible way to return:
well, I mean, that's simply not cricket!

I knew that it would take a long time,
if mankind was to make a great mark,
but I didn't realise how final it was,
that day when I'd turned up to embark.

We're to be the first of our species
to land on Mars – that's our true fate,
and if we survive our arrival,
our next job will be to pro-create!

Now I've had a look round at the rest of the crew,
and there's none I'd want go out with on a date,
so it could be a long, lonely existence
if I'm the only one not taking a mate.

There's one girl who's been looking at me,
and paying me lots of attention,
I think I know what's on her agenda,
I think I can spot her intention!

So here I am, trapped in this spaceship,
with only the Sun's gravity to tow it,
heading off to a fate worse than death –
it's space, Jim, but not as we know it.

Ah yes – the MPs in the Mother of Parliaments, and their well-publicised "expenses scandal". I'd like to think it was a one-off thing, and that they've tightened up the rules a lot. But it just keeps on happening. Together with "cash for questions" and lobbying scandals.

<u>Snouts In The Trough</u>

It's good that we live in in a democracy,
With flags blazing and banners uncurled;
Here in the Mother of Parliaments -
An example we hold out to the world.

And we take this stuff damned seriously:
We're not mere amateur hobbyists,
But now we've taken our eye off the ball,
And let in the canker of lobbyists.

But it takes two to tango they say,
Someone who needs a question to be asked,
And someone whose position is privileged,
With a streak of greed that's thinly masked.

There's a lack of transparency
In this access for cash
Their action is rash
Trying to look flash
As they sit in a sash
Making a huge mash
And principles into trash.

Where's honesty and integrity gone?
Public service in office?
It's gone down the abyss
They're taking the piss
By behaving like this
Let's give them a hiss
Tell them to kiss
Their cushy jobs good-bye.

Only hidden cameras and microphones
Have blown this thing open -
Insider access is a wheeze
They start with a tease

Then outline their fees
Soon acting with ease
They should be on their knees
Not slopping in grease
And wallowing in sleaze.

And to add insult to the injury,
By using these tools, they take us for fools,
And with faces all innocently turned,
Claim "I was only following the rules!"

Is nothing sacred? Well the Royal Mail is obviously not. Through progressive privatisations, and the political dogma of "market forces", one of our national institutions was put up for sale.

Mail for Sale

Looks like the end of an era,
But I'm not drinking a toast -
They've sold off everything else,
And now it's the turn of the Post.

They'll give the postmen a pay-rise,
And bribe them all with free shares.
It's like they don't give a toss any more;
It's as if nobody cares!

It's not the service that counts any more,
But the profits the investors are after,
With our protests not likely to be heard,
Over the sound of their laughter.

It won't be for the public's benefit,
So don't be surprised by what you get:
Things'll get worse, rather than better,
I think we should be willing to bet.

In private hands it just won't be the same,
In the ownership of these go-getters,
And we'll find we haven't got a clue,
About who's handling our letters.

Goodbye to EiiR on the post-box,
And farewell to old Postman Pat:
There'll be no room for duffers like him,
Nor for his black-and-white cat.

Goodbye to the royal insignia -
I suppose all that stuff will be dead.
They'll come up with some fancy new colour,
And there'll be no more Post Office Red.

Goodbye to the little vans in the lane:
There'll be no more of our friendly old postie -

A figure from the age of the Penny Black,
A memory, like an old ghostie.

Soon they'll stop the daily collections,
Down into the town we'll all have to tramp.
They'll charge us for every delivery,
And ramp up the price of a stamp.

Is there nothing sacred these days?
Is everything destined to fail?
No – you can't depend on anything,
Once they've sold off our Royal Mail.

We did have a hot Summer – once. Then everybody complained that it was too damned hot! There's no pleasing some people.

My God But It's Hot

The flags on the flagpoles hang limp
The air's as dry as sandpaper
The Earth's turning back into dust
And as the mercury climbs
All my energy's shot
I'm sweating a lot
My God, but it's hot!

The lawn has turned brown and yellow
And patches have died quite away
The veggies are wilted and small
The Test Match goes on uninterrupted
The heatwave goes on and on
Pleasant it's not
In fact it's quite grot
My God, but it's hot!

Everyone's stripping off & perspiring
We're getting through gallons of sunscreen
But still our skin's burning
The Sun's a bright disc in the sky
Almost like a red dot
I'm sure it's a dark plot
My God, but it's hot!

The temperature is just "Scorchio"
In French it's "tres chaud"
In German "sehr heiss"
It could be in Fahrenheit
It might be in Centrigade
The thermometer's shot
I don't know what's what
My God, but it's hot!

The forecast holds no relief
And reservoirs are wasting away
There'll soon be an end to sprinklers
And a ban on the use of hosepipes

Then the ground will turn to powder
And whatever we've got
Even fresh food will rot
My God, but it's hot!

The fans toil away regardless
But there's no cooling relief
Yet this is only a Summer
It's the thing that we wanted!
The Winter will be back soon enough
I care not a jot
For that is our lot
My God, but it's hot!

A major news story a few years ago was that one of the main London sewers had been blocked by a huge build-up of fatty deposits, referred to in the press as a "fatberg". It didn't make for pleasant reading. I imagined what it must have been like to be called out to deal with such a problem.

<u>Fatberg</u>

We got the emergency call at night,
and we headed out there at first light.
He'd said *"there seems to be a blockage I think –*
we were alerted by the terrible stink".
Our brave men soon climbed under the ground,
and were frankly amazed at what they soon found:
the sewage had swelled up into a great ball,
went right up to the ceiling and wall-to-wall.

It was the biggest obstruction we'd seen,
and to tackle it, nobody was keen.
It looked like the worst project from hell,
and that doesn't even cover the smell.
We named it the fatberg – just for a joke –
but it weren't funny when we started to poke,
to discover of what it was made,
and tried to dislodge it with a sharp spade.

It consisted of fat and congealed grease,
then wet-wipes and nappies were the next piece.
Sanitary towels was one of the thirds,
and the rest was an assortment of turds.
You see, people go to the loo in a rush,
and give not a care to whatever they flush.
It's a general waste disposal can:
they tend to forget once it's gone down the pan.

But I digress, for disposal was now the task.
How did we shift it? I'm hearing you ask.
Well, lend an ear and don't be too gobby,
and I'll tell you how we shifted that jobbie.
The thing was enormous that was for sure:
we had to get on top to effect a cure.
A man had to ascend, using crampons,
and ropes to clamber over the tampons.

We pulled and tugged it from the crown,
and even considered melting it down.
We used hammers and drills of all types,
and attacked it with axes and hosepipes.
The thing wouldn't yield, resisted the assault.
We tried everything, but it wasn't our fault,
and we realised the thing was stuck tight,
then we resorted to dynamite.

It was only meant to be a small blast,
but once we'd started, the die it was cast.
We weren't sure how far off we should walk,
but it was like a bottle blowing its cork.
You see the sewer's narrow like a funnel,
so all of the debris shot down the tunnel.
We were in the way – that's the truth of it;
not surprising that we got covered in shit.

We were well messy, if you get my drift,
but at least it was in blocks we could shift.
As a workforce we looked sad and sorry,
but we loaded it all up on a lorry.
So next time you think you might go for a piss,
listen closely and reflect upon this:
It's a nice moral I think that you'll find:
out of sight ain't the same as out of mind.

The UK Government approved the culling of badgers in Gloucestershire and Somerset. But the marksmen they employed failed to hit their targets. I mean they didn't shoot "enough" badgers to make a measurable difference. And the incidence of bovine TB did not decline. Following the howls of public protest to the culls in the first place, there were then howls of government bungling and inefficiency. The excuse given by Government's Environment Minister Owen Paterson for this failure was that "the badgers had moved the goal-posts". You couldn't make this stuff up.

Goalposts

There's something odd going on in the night,
And I don't think it's the action of ghosts,
I think I might have rumbled the culprits,
'Cos it's the badgers what's moving the goalposts.

They're fed up of being cast as the bad guys;
They say that they're not even criminal types,
But they're being pushed into a corner,
Just because of their black and white stripes.

They're not playing for Newcastle United,
Nor other league teams out on the coasts.
They don't want to be blamed as the scapegoats,
And that's why the badgers are moving the goalposts.

They've had enough of government ministers,
The farmers, and other tub-thumpers,
They're confused by all the statistics,
And the constant re-hashing of numbers.

So now they've called on all of their allies,
All the creatures that the countryside boasts,
And got them to sabotage the hunting,
Whilst they get on with moving more goalposts.

What if the deer changed all of the white markings,
And the foxes built a new ditch?
What if the rats ran off with the corner flags,
And the field-mice built nests on the pitch?

What if the cats and rats infested the grand-stands,
And the kestrels ruled over all as the hosts?
Then the biggest change that you'd see on the ground,
Wouldn't be the badgers moving the goalposts.

Bad science is causing this mayhem;
But it shouldn't cause much of a shock,
Because this is what you'll end up with,
If you keep putting Mr. Brock in the dock.

So let's get this cull into perspective:
Let's not celebrate victory with toasts.
Let's understand that it's all a big mess -
It's the badgers moving the goalposts!

Bit of a shock to find out a few years back that Charles, Prince of Wales, had reached the grand old age of sixty-five – and he still hadn't ascended to the throne. Jolly good.

<u>One Is Sixty-Five</u>

Thank-you so much! One is delighted!
One is so grateful – it's really a gas,
with the nation in so much of a mess,
to finally get hold of One's bus-pass!

One's not sure what it's used for,
but One feels it must be a very great perk,
although One previously understood,
that One qualified *after* doing the work?

See – One's still waiting to get on with the job,
a situation that's a bit rummy,
(it's a question of royal succession -
we have to settle the problem of Mummy).

One loves her, of course, and also the Greek –
naturally, One is terribly loyal –
but One has been hanging around for a bit now,
and One is still not the senior royal.

One has kept Oneself quietly occupied,
carrying out visits as a mere filler,
there was that *gel* Diana, at One time,
but just lately One has been with Camilla.

One has tried to do One's regal duty,
producing young Wills as One's heir,
but just in case of any mishaps,
One has provided Harry as the spare.

But there's only so much time One can spend,
at Highgrove, One earnestly feels.
Sixty-five years is far too much time,
for anyOne to be kicking One's heels.

One's had enough of Duchy Originals,
One finds that the time drags and pales,

One asks - just how long is long enough,
to still be the blessed Prince of Wales?

One dabbles in homeopathy,
and One has to be patient, One grants,
but One finds that after so many years,
One has long conversations with One's plants.

One rattles between Windsor and Balmoral,
but the servants are getting bored and callous,
and are starting to wonder if their master,
will ever command the corgis at Buck Palace.

One has to remain interested,
One has to look as if One is still keen,
but we've had the Diamond Jubilee now –
why does the parent still want to be queen?

Surely it's time to let some-One else have a go?
One doesn't know what else One could do,
but to carry on hoping and waiting,
to keep standing here in this short queue.

And what do you do? How interesting!
One must keep Oneself busy - that's the thing!
But One looks like One will get a free TV Licence,
before One finally gets to be king!

The original Monty Python team got back together for a few shows. By their own admission they didn't do it for fun, or for old times' sake, but for the money. Bit disappointing really.

Something Completely Different

The long wait is finally over,
it was the full two decade argument,
but they've managed to get it together,
and the Pythons have decided to relent.

All of them might now be in their seventies,
and it may be just a financial wheeze,
but Gilliam, Idle and Palin,
are coming back with Jones and with Cleese.

Of course Graham Chapman couldn't make it,
for obvious reasons we know to be true:
for some years now he's been "just resting",
like the old famous Norwegian Blue.

Yes he's shuffled off this mortal coil,
after too many years of getting pissed.
He's deceased, and gone to meet his maker,
he is no more, he's ceased to exist.

So the rest will carry on without him,
and hope that they can all get along,
but some sketches just won't be the same –
take for instance The Lumberjack Song.

The Gumbys and the Piranha Brothers,
Harry "Snapper" Organs of Q Division,
Spiny Norman, a man with three buttocks,
and nobody expects The Spanish Inquisition.

The Popular Front of Judea,
Knights that go "Nimh", and all of that jam,
an Albatross, and Every Sperm Is Sacred,
all served up with Spam, Egg & Chips…and Spam!

The Life of Brian, mocking religion,
playing word-games both clever and coy,
always Looking On The Bright Side of Life,
not being evil, just a Very Naughty Boy.

The Upper Class Twit of The Year Show,
a Holy Grail, and sketches both daft and plucky:
we loved The Ministry of Silly Walks,
back in those golden days "We Were Lucky!"

Anyway, they say they've settled their differences,
it'll be a golden payday that's hard to begrudge,
the latest revival of a dead parrot,
not so much "wink, wink", as "nudge, nudge".

Whatever is their motivation,
let's just hope that they're not going to fail:
for me, It's……. great comedy gold,
The Meaning of Life, and The Holy Grail.

Celebrating the opening of the first pub on Britain's motorway network at Beaconsfield on the M40. Whose bright idea was this?

One For The Road

I was just trundlin' down to London,
and, feelin' tired, I fancied a rest,
but what met my eyes at Beaconsfield,
was more than I ever could have guessed.

I pulled off the road, into the car park,
and started looking for tea and some grub,
when I noticed The Hope & Champion:
I couldn't believe it – there was a pub!

Now I'm as fond of a pint as the next man,
and reaching a watering-hole so soon,
appeared like a mirage in the desert,
courtesy that nice Mr Wetherspoon!

I've no truck with spirits or alcopops,
and drinking and driving are sinful,
but a swift half of excellent beer,
is quite a long way from a skin-full.

So I settled down for a drink at the bar,
ignored all the bottles and ordered a half,
but the barmaid said I had to be jokin',
such short measures – was I havin' a laugh?

I suppose it's just their sales tactics,
for she told me her name to be Carole,
but she wasn't really very attractive –
for looks, she was scrapin' the barrel.

But a woman's allure can't be discounted,
she knew how to peddle the pub's wares,
she talked and charmed me, really quite calmed me,
and soon I'd forgotten all of my cares.

And thus it was I ordered a full glass,
sure that it wasn't enough to be boozy,
but, what with fatigue and strength of the ale,
I soon started to feel rather woozy.

I have to admit that it was a strange pint,
not a flavour I'd encountered before,
rather gassy, and a bit fruity,
but a pint was enough: I couldn't have more.

Now there's nothing droll, about alcohol,
I knew that some fresh air was the way,
soon I could feel, I was fine behind the wheel,
so headed back out onto the Motorway.

For safety, I decided to take things slow,
keep to the speed limit, and the centre lane,
I took no notice of other motorists,
nor the black car that had started to gain.

I was now happily drivin' along,
but tiredness I was having to fight,
it wasn't the sirens that woke me up,
but the strength of that blue flashing light.

They pulled me into the hard shoulder,
the constable came over, and said with a wink,
*"I'm sadly grieving, to notice you weaving,
but is it possible you've had a drink?"*

I admitted the pint I'd had just before,
I said I didn't lead the life of a monk,
I knew that he'd caught me, whilst on the M40,
but was sure I couldn't nearly be drunk.

The police-man was quite nice about it,
tho' he had to give me the breathalyzer.
He was quite frank – it was totally blank,
for Carole had only been feeding me Tizer.

It was reported a couple of years ago that sales of porridge oats were to be the highest for many years. Is this the sign of our recession-hit times?

Doing Porridge

They've found it in the long-dead stomachs
of ancient peat-bog dwellers so old,
for it's a very durable substance,
once it's set and allowed to go cold.
Scraps of it still adhere to kitchen walls,
where a pan of it once exploded,
and it carries many a memory,
once it's been analysed and de-coded.

It's a reminder of times quite distant,
a material that's said to be fissile,
and, once rolled into a tight little ball,
it can even be used as a missile.
Now this food-stuff's something of a winner,
and its utility takes some beating,
for it's popular North of the Border:
a Scottish substitute for Central Heating.

Yes - I speak of a dish of hot porridge:
high in fibre, vitamins and protein,
it lowers cholesterol and blood pressure,
a meal that's fit for a queen.
A humble bowl is so full of goodness,
low in sugar and easy digestible,
not like one of your fancy breakfasts,
but a food that's a wholesome comestible.

It's much better than a full English,
yoghurt, muesli or hominy grits.
It tastes much smoother too,
because it doesn't come with the bits.
It's not fishy like old kippers,
nor crunchy like you get with fruit and with nuts.
It slides down all soft and seductive,
then it sticks to the sides of your guts.

But you have to make it the true way,
neither too heavy, nor too light,
neither too hot nor too cold,
if you want it to be just about right.
Oatmeal and water and some salt
is the method that really rocks,
and then you must stir it all clockwise,
if you want it to suit Goldilocks.

For the stirring keeps the Devil away,
and forces him to run and to hurtle,
and if that doesn't seem to work,
you can despatch him with the spurtle.
Tho' it's Scottish, it don't use a sheep's stomach,
so from this dish there's no need to hide.
You don't need to eat it with Irn-Bru,
and, unlike Mars bars, it's not even deep-fried.

They sell it in Prêt -a-Manger to take away,
and even McDonalds are in on the game.
So there must be profits in oatmeal,
but it's good for you all the same.
It may be a guard against cold weather,
but here's the point – if you want to take notes:
they say it's an aphrodisiac –
so there's more than one way of getting your oats.

Having had prostate cancer myself, I'm very aware of the risks of this disease. "Movember" is one of those awareness-raising campaigns I usually participate in, with varying degrees of success in the facial hair department.

By A Whisker

Remember, Remember, now it's November,
It's time that we all had a bash,
Time to think of men's prostate charities,
And had a go at growing a moustache!

This ain't a task to be taken lightly,
To be altering your features so facial,
Especially when starting from scratch,
And the rate of production is glacial.

It can change your appearance quite sudden,
As the first fluff appears on the lip,
But it takes longer than you might at first think,
Before, with scissors, you're ready to snip.

So while you're waiting for the bristles to grow,
You can anticipate what might appear beneath,
Along that delicate, thin strip of skin,
Between your nose, and your lips and your teeth.

You start with a stencil, the shape of a pencil,
Then, as it becomes lush, more like a bush,
You can raise the bar to greater ambition,
Till you've got something more like a toothbrush.

Then you can start piling and styling,
It's not too taxing, while you're relaxing,
You feel like a Charley, and look something like Dali,
But that requires much more curling and waxing.

Then your style can get more creative:
There's lots you can do, with hair that's all new:
You could go far, with a large handlebar,
Or train it to look like Fu Manchu.

You'd look no fatter, with a Zapata,
A Mexican style that looks pretty dapper,
Careful engraving, done whilst you're shaving,
And you'll end up looking like Frank Zappa.

If you've material, to grow an Imperial,
And you can do this without any fuss,
Then you're well on your way to celebrity,
And will soon resemble a walrus.

When you've got there, you can say that you've made it;
You can afford to be all cock-a-hoop:
Remember the greatest use for a moustache
Is something for straining your soup!

Early in 2014 scientists re-awoke the Rosetta probe in deep space, ready to begin its mission to attempt a landing on a comet, a venture in which they later succeeded. I envisaged this event as if it were a reluctant teenager being told that it was time to get up.

Awakening

It's bad enough that they've sent me out here,
within the deep, dark frontiers of space,
in some wide-ranging lonely orbit,
'cos out near Jupiter's a damned dingy place.

Worse – they've left me to float inactive,
beyond home planets, out here in the deep,
but now they've had the gall and damned cheek,
expect me to just wake up from my sleep.

They sit there back at home in some comfort,
saying *"Time to wake up, Rosetta!"*
after I've been snoozing for nearly two years:
to be honest – I wish I felt better.

I just want to hit the snooze button,
to silence this intruding alarm,
to stop this electronic ringing,
shut the damn thing up, to get back to calm.

But hibernation's no longer allowed:
seems I've got to spring into action,
and get my antennae and boosters shifting –
they want to continue the transaction.

There's a task I'm programmed to complete,
an endeavour I just can't avoid,
the transmission said *"complete your mission:
time to start chasing that asteroid!"*

It's a dangerous, elliptical task,
with a flight-path light-years beyond Mars.
I know I'll vomit when I get near the comet,
but if I miss, I'll be out there in the stars.

How I wish I could come back home again,
where I was made, the place of my birth.
I've found it's no fun, out here near the Sun –
please! Can't I return to the Earth?

Or at least let me return to my slumbers,
let me go back to the realm of my dreams,
find some other bundle of hardware,
to accomplish your plans and your schemes!

Let me re-fold my solar panels,
let my circuits cool down and then,
if I just ignore my own software,
I could get back to sleep once again.

Just let me pull back over my covers,
for this task I wish I hadn't been built.
Can't we just say I'm having a duvet day,
as I sink under my electronic quilt?

So if you lot think you've got a hard life,
as you struggle to stifle a yawn,
just think of me out here in deep space,
next time the alarm clock goes off in the dawn.

I'll be out here chasing the comet's tail,
although I'm told at the end of this test,
as my new ongoing incentive,
they're going to let me have a VERY long rest!

A CHRISTMAS SELECTION BOX

I'll be honest - I hate Christmas.   And New Year. With a vengeance, bordering on paranoia. It's not some deep psychological scarring that I've carried through life from having had a bad time as a child. In fact, I have fond memories of Christmas when I was young, when I still believed in Santa Claus. (What do you mean – of course he really exists! Doesn't he?). No - my dislike has built up over the years (another side-effect of aging and developing curmudgeon-ness I suppose). Apart from all the rampant consumerism and all that goes with it, there are two things that really get up my nose – the fact that it seems to start earlier every year (Christmas menus go up in July in my local pub), and the whole month or so of disruption that a simple two-day Bank Holiday can induce. Same with New Year, and all the pressure to "celebrate" and (help me) "have a good time". Where is the box I can tick to opt out of this annual season of misery?

This section contains poems that I have performed many times between early December and mid-January. If you really love Christmas I suggest you might want to skip this section.

A Crash In The Woods

Sometime late, deep in the middle of the night,
Something woke me from slumber's deep delight:
A whoosh, a wallop, a screech and a big loud bang,
Thunder and lightning, and an almighty clang,
Then a pause, silence, almost nothing at all,
Followed by an explosion, a boom, a fireball -
It sounded like the crash of an airplane,
Crack, then all quiet, then crack all over again.

I ran to the window, and looked into the dark -
It was cold, and starlit, and all of that lark.
It was hard to make out, I couldn't see all that good,
But it seemed as if something had come down in the wood,
Something was burning, a great tower of flame -
I needed to get out there, this wasn't no game,
So I pulled on my clothes, and made for the scene -
It was an emergency, you know what I mean?

The site of the accident was pretty easy to find,
A scene of destruction of every possible kind.
It was hard to know where I should start,
But in the midst was what remained of a cart,
Blown to bits, scattered every which way,
What could only be described as the remains of a sleigh,
With smoking and burning bits of debris -
A helluva smash had occurred, it was easy to see.

The bloke that had been driving was stuck up a tree,
And from his red and white outfit he struggled to get free,
So I helped to get him down, along with his sack.
His face and beard were all burnt nearly black,
He smouldered and sizzled, he was in a right state
Berating his rotten luck and cursing his fate,
His looks and his temper were really not sweet,
And his language was far too foul to repeat.

There was fear and panic written all over his face,
And barbecued reindeer running all over the place,
There were parcels and packages spread all about,
And small green elves, crying, and starting to shout -

A small-scale disaster so deep in the woods,
Meant that Santa would fail to deliver his goods,
So I asked if there was anything I could possibly do,
To which Santa replied *"I think I'm buggered, don't you?"*

I thought he was worried about the waiting girls and boys,
If he didn't turn up at their houses to deliver their toys,
But he said that was the least of his worries,
It was bound to happen to a chap that always hurries.
He'd be in big trouble with the delivery firm -
They'd be sure to bring his contract to term:
To his sacking this situation was obviously leading,
And the police'd figure out he'd been speeding.

"It's this zero-hours contract that's to blame:
Too many deliveries to make – it's a loser's game!
I've got to do every blessed thing, all in one day,
And all they give me is eight-reindeer-power sleigh!
It's relentless, and there's no breaks for meals!
It's simply awful – you've no idea how it feels!
Now they're gonna catch me all bang to rights,
I just knew it would happen one of these Christmas nights!"

I felt sorry for him – he was pitiful and very forlorn,
And I couldn't do much to help him, but I was torn -
He was a victim of our modern capitalist culture,
Working for a firm that was an asset-stripping vulture,
So I helped him round up the reindeer and the elves,
Told them to grab what they wanted, just help themselves,
Then I took him back to my place that was close by,
And gave him a sherry and a mince pie.

Now I'm not relating all this just for some fun,
But don't worry – my tale's almost over and done,
There's a happy ending to this miserable verse!
You know – things could have been much worse –
They cleared up the crash, and Santa's out on probation.
He took it easy for a while, then had a vacation,
Got himself sorted out and jumped back on the horse,
And now he's a delivery driver for ParcelForce!

How We Know It's Nearly Christmas

How we know it's nearly Christmas?
Advent calendars and all of that -
the turkeys are getting very nervous,
and the ducks and geese are getting fat.

How we know it's nearly Christmas?
Sudden sightings of Santa and his pals,
in every shop and department store,
and sightings of elves walking round the malls.

How we know it's nearly Christmas?
Markets flooded with celebrity tomes,
men disappearing into their lofts,
and putting light-bulbs on the *outside* of homes.

How we know it's nearly Christmas?
A frantic, nervous spirit intervenes,
and though the weather's overcast and grey,
the store displays show only snowy scenes.

How we know it's nearly Christmas?
There's a wealth of special treats and sights,
a sudden burst of German markets,
and D-List celebs switching on a few lights.

How we know it's nearly Christmas?
For the non-religious it's slim pickings,
a bizarre interest in ghost stories,
and everything dressed up to look like Dickens!

How we know it's nearly Christmas?
Transport timetables fall into a mess:
they're offering special bargains,
and there's a discount sale at DFS!

How we know it's nearly Christmas?
We're told that children are all a-glow,
there's a nasty outbreak of tinsel,
and everything's covered up in fake snow.

How we know it's nearly Christmas?
Of comfort and joy there must be tiding,
we're on constant loop tapes of Slade,
and men called Noel are going in to hiding.

How we know it's nearly Christmas?
There's lots false jollity and ho-ho-ho,
there's satsumas and brazil nuts everywhere,
a man dressed as Santa sits in his grotto.

How we know it's nearly Christmas?
TV channels devoted to hard-sell,
closing and posting times are all different,
every ad is accompanied by sleigh-bells.

How we know it's nearly Christmas?
We're all exhorted to be of good cheer,
everyone's searching for good presents,
and check-out girls wear reindeer headgear.

How we know it's nearly Christmas?
Trees on the pavement, discounted games,
book early for your Summer holiday,
and men wearing make-up, dressed up as dames.

How we know it's nearly Christmas?
The Marketing machine's telling its tale.
Anyway – I'm off round to Tesco's:
their Easter eggs have just gone back on sale.

Interview For Job Of Santa Claus

Welcome to our store, dear gentlemen,
If you could please form an orderly queue.
We've lots of interviews scheduled,
But we'll get round to talk to all of you.

Please hand in your Curricu-Claus Vitae,
As you enter the room through the doors,
And we'll get on with the process
Of picking this Christmas's Santa Claus.

Of course there'll be lots of questions,
We have to be careful who we employ,
For we've found it's not just anyone,
That can spread tidings of comfort and joy.

The job description's a bit wider this year,
As the recession continues to bite:
We're expecting much more from our Santa -
We're determined to get our choice right.

So there'll be lots of questions to answer,
As we try to get right to the root,
Of who's the very best candidate,
And before we hand over the fat suit.

For example: do you have experience
Of being seated for many long hours?
Are you possessed of rosy-cheekedness?
And is cheerfulness within your powers?

It's more than just being good with children,
And dealing with all those little cuties,
For you'll have to muck out the reindeer,
And carry out Elf liaison duties.

You'll be working with height-challenged workers,
Cos Elf & Safety's a modern-day fact,
And seasonal work isn't much of a perk,
For it's only a limited contract.

You'll need "Toddler Expectation Management",
Cos some of their parents can be real rough!
Do you have a current sleigh-driving licence?
Otherwise this role's gonna be real tough.

For, dealing with demanding children,
You must be brave and not be a-feared.
Do you have enough roly-poly-ness,
And do you think you could grow your own beard?

We'll need your face crinkling, and your eyes twinkling,
A constant yo-ho-ho you'll have to do.
You can't have a bad back, if you're to carry that sack,
And do red-and-white colours suit you?

You'll be part of the retail experience,
Thus extracting the parental dime,
And there's through-put targets to be met,
So each child gets limited knee-time.

You've got to be endlessly cheerful,
But work-place sobriety is our motto -
You can't go out and get yourself beer-full -
Nobody gets blotto in our grotto!

Cos though there's many temptations,
From all the bottles and beer barrels,
You'll have to find another way to block out
The endless loop-tape of Christmas carols.

They say "don't work with animals and children" -
Normally we'd endorse this as a rule,
But if one of you doesn't take this job,
Nobody's gonna have much of a Yule.

Nativity

Nostalgia ain't what it used to be,
But I can't help thinking of that day,
Right at the back end of the Fifties,
When I did my first Nativity Play.

We were in the first class of the Infants,
Young and innocent, no more than five or six,
When our teacher announced the production,
And we'd all be thrown into the mix.

There were to be parts for everyone,
Of that fact there should be no doubt,
For the school couldn't cope with the aggro,
If any of the class were to be left out.

For parents would want to see their darlings,
Deep in the Christmas story engage,
Showing off to their friends and relatives,
Of their first public performance on stage.

None of us knew what to expect,
Because none of us had ever done it before,
But if we couldn't have a major role,
We decided we didn't want to play any more.

I didn't get to play Joseph,
And the role of inn-keeper to me was denied,
I finally ended up as fifth shepherd,
I was so upset that I cried.

My mum thought my skill had been ignored,
And my talent not allowed to shine through,
Which just added to the misery,
But I was only five – what could I do?

Rehearsals were more than chaotic,
The teachers didn't know how to lead,
And scripts were a complete waste of time,
Since not one of us could read.

So we did it by practising quite hard,
Repeating scenes over and over again,
Learning lines was a complete nightmare,
We were children trying to play men.

There was no proper stage to speak of,
You could see it was heading for a great fall,
So they just draped a large pair of curtains,
Right across one end of the hall.

Costumes were left up to the parents,
For each to interpret as they chose,
With no attempt to co-ordinate,
We ended with an array of odd clothes.

The shepherds used sheets and tea-towels,
There were cardboard gold crowns for the kings,
The Angel Gabriel was a fantastic sight,
Dwarfed by a pair of white paper wings.

Moustaches were drawn with burnt cork,
And false beards stuck on that were itchy,
Nobody could really see what they were doing,
And the inn-keeper's wife turned a touch bitchy.

Joseph wore specs and a belted tunic,
Mary appeared in virginal white,
As they stumbled into Bethlehem,
And inaudibly asked for a room for the night.

The innkeeper, over-awed by the audience,
Forgot his lines and burst into tears.
Lots of shuffling at the edge of the stage,
Then the fulfilment of our worst fears.

The baby donkey, hired for the occasion,
Peed on stage, as we'd all hoped that he would:
A large pool spread between his feet,
And surrounded the cast where they stood.

You couldn't get away from the squelching,
Though the actors were never in danger,
But most of the dialogue was lost,
As ox and ass waded into the manger.

The gold, the frankincense and myrrh,
Were dropped on to the swaddled-up child,
But the rising smell of fresh urine,
Was driving the audience wild.

At this point, the star fell from its perch,
And knocked the Angel Gabriel out cold.
The girls and boys started wailing,
And mayhem ensued, it has to be told.

The head teacher appeared with bucket and mop,
Halting proceedings with a bilious wince.
That brought an end to my acting career,
And I've hated Christmas ever since!

A New Christmas Carol

Christmas comes but once a year,
So let's thank the Lord for that.
The turkeys are becoming nervous,
And the geese are getting fat.

There's fake snow everywhere,
And decorations that look tired.
Whilst down at the Job Centre
Some Santas are getting hired.

For it's that season of good cheer,
With yuletide adverts day and night,
But with early carol-singers
It's hard to get a Silent Night.

The season starts sooner every year:
In the shops they're already selling holly.
But with all these Christmas jingles about,
I'm finding it hard to keep things jolly.

In the gloomy shopping precinct,
They've put up the civic lights.
But it's hard to start getting all yo-ho-ho,
When there's still some weeks till holy night.

And in the shops they've got yuletide offers,
With Santa sitting in his grotto,
Selling booze at half the price,
With the promise that we'll all get blotto.

With new ideas for Christmas gifts,
Re-packaging of every blessed thing,
And people buying presents -
Hark! - the herald cash-tills sing.

But Yule can be a lonely time,
Especially for those still single,
Serving to remind them of their state,
With every irritating jingle.

TV adverts showing happy families,
Like some cosy scene in Dickens,
Gathered round a roaring fire,
Whilst we shop online like headless chickens.

Once in Bristol's Royal City,
You could hear a festive carol.
The prices have gone up till January:
They've got us over a barrel.

So deck the halls with boughs of holly,
And ding-dong merrily on high.
When you've spent more than you can afford,
It's getting time to question why.

Good King Wenceslas didn't have to go shopping,
Even on the Feast of Stephen.
So why do we have to try so hard,
When we're fighting to break even?

It's all got very mixed up these days:
I think there's quite a danger
Of having three TV pundits
Voting to put reindeer in the manger.

You can't make a snowman out of rain or sleet,
Nor find three wise men to employ.
There's no good reason to be cheerful,
Nothing to bring tidings of comfort and joy.

God rest ye merry gentlemen,
But you know it's not very funny.
It's no longer a celebration,
It's just about the money.

And *"do they know it's Christmas?"*
Is a song you'll probably sing.
But it's not just about Africa
Do *we* really know what we're doing?

But I suppose I should have greater cheer,
And stop with all this huffing,
So now I'll just say *"Bah humbug!"*
And *"could you pass the stuffing?"*

The Icing On The Cake

It was Christmas Eve in the kitchen,
Everything prepared, everything nice.
The turkey was stuffed and the veggies peeled,
So there was only the cake left to ice.

But I'd left it to the last minute,
And there wasn't time to nip to the shop.
It was easy enough to make icing,
But nothing to decorate the top.

So my husband went out to his shed,
To see what he might be able to find,
And came back with a jar of ball-bearings,
Saying: "*who's to know? Nobody will mind.*"

So I washed them and polished them bright,
Though it was all a bit of a fiddle,
And I placed them right round the edges,
With a sprig of holly in the middle.

Well, it looked proper champion,
With the large silver balls catching the light.
When my mother-in-law came the next day,
She'd be bound to admire the sight.

Well, Christmas Day came, and lovely it was,
We had our dinner, and a good drink,
Then mother-in-law eyed up the cake,
And said: "*I'll have a piece of that I think*".

So we both looked, and smothered a smile,
And with a knife I cut her a large slice.
She ate it up quickly and smacked her lips,
Saying: "*that was really quite nice!*"

"*I'll have another piece if you please!*"
And that disappeared as fast as the first,
And then we all had a few more drinks,
As we'd all developed a thirst.

114

At this stage we were all stuffed to the gills.
The fire in the grate had burned down quite low,
So mother-in-law picked up the poker,
To stir it around and build up a glow.

Now we'd been eating and drinking all day:
Stuffing, and sprouts, and peas that were tinned,
And what with the turkey and the beer,
Well, it were bound to give the girl wind.

As she leaned and bent herself forward,
And, bearing in mind that she were quite fat,
She farted out bearings with incredible force,
And loudly assassinated the cat.

The Theft Of Baby Jesus

There's always some-one who goes too far,
Whose judgement seems somewhat defective,
Getting Christmas all out of proportion,
And losing their sense of perspective.

The bloke in our village was one of these:
Went over the top for Noel-time tradition,
Thought the number of lights on his house,
Was some sort of yearly competition.

He had everything on display,
Such a mess, it was really a sin:
A complete mish-mash of every sort,
Every blessed thing that you might imagine.

There was Santa with all twelve of his reindeer,
Delivering presents piled up on his sleigh.
It took so many bulbs to light up this scene,
You'd have thought night had turned into day.

There were snow-men and snow-women,
Cartoon characters, the holly and ivy,
Illustrations of every blessed carol,
And tunes in a tape-loop to keep it all lively.

This guy was more than a fanatic -
Of under-statement there was no danger:
And his central tableau showed a great star,
Hovering over the scene in the manger.

There were Mary and Joseph in the stable,
With the Holy Infant, shepherds and then,
A hovering Angel of The Lord,
And a gathering of the three wise men.

And there were great piles of presents,
As if no detail could be allowed to pass,
Every type of farm-yard animal,
Not merely the ox and the ass.

A twenty-foot Christmas tree capped off the scene,
Which became a local attraction,
And the passing traffic became so bad,
That we decided we had to take action.

A group of us hatched our plot in the pub,
Which is not the best place to think straight,
But it seemed a good idea at the time,
When we'd had a few, and the hour got late.

The plan was to hit him where it hurt,
Something to make that daft bugger feel.
We were going to remove Baby Jesus,
Yes! – the Son of Man we plotted to steal.

We decided we'd hold Him to ransom,
And that, as the fruit of our labours,
He'd then scale down the size of his display,
And we'd be the toast of his neighbours.

We thought it'd be the simplest of raids,
To sneak in among that barrage of light,
To just steal the youthful Son of Man,
And disappear back into the night.

But we counted without so many wires,
That would cause us so many glitches -
The complex inter-connectedness,
The circuits and timers and switches.

Electricity don't mix with stupidity –
We were pissed (to use the vernacular),
And as we made our grab for the infant,
The meltdown was truly spectacular.

Our theft was far from deft,
Taking the hostage created a ruction.
The air became blue, as the fuses all blew,
And that was the end of abduction.

The lights went out all over the house,
As the circuits became overloaded,
And there was a short-term glow in the sky,
As the whole of the creation exploded.

Then in the street and the village,
There was an end to illumination.
It carried on all down the valley,
And finally blew up the sub-station.

It was a case of a simple crime gone wrong,
And in later years, folks were heard to say,
It made a great change from the usual -
The most spectacular one-off display!

Post Natal Depression (or thank goodness Christmas is all over)

They've all gone back to work,
And the kids are back at school.
Here I am in the middle of all the mess,
Clearing up like a bloody fool.

And as I look around and survey the site,
In the fireplace there's a fall of soot,
An empty sherry glass and mince-pie crumbs,
And a mark where Santa placed his foot.

The carrots we left for his reindeer,
Have been quite nibbled away,
But the droppings on the carpet,
I think is a price too high to pay.

There's paper wrap and discarded boxes,
Where presents were pulled out in their haste,
Played with for half an hour,
Before joining the rest of the waste.

There's food left over in the kitchen,
And I think I'm starting to droop.
If I have to eat one more leftover sprout,
Or face another bowl of turkey soup.

The Christmas tree is looking all forlorn,
As its needles drop upon the floor,
And get blown around the house,
Every time someone opens a door.

We've started our own recycling skip,
With empty bottles of every sort.
It's not just the beer and the mixers,
But the gin, the vodka and port.

We've watched all of the Christmas specials
They put on the box this time of the year.
Shame they can't do it the rest of the season,
Instead of the usual rubbish so drear.

We've sent home the old relatives
Those aged wonderful old dears.
Now it's time to take down the greetings cards,
From people we've not seen in years.

We'll take down the lights that cover the house.
Our neighbours think that we're soft.
Yes, we'll pack up the baubles and lights,
And put them all back in the loft.

The sparkle's all gone from the occasion,
All the drinking and eating and that.
They've stopped playing Christmas records on the radio:
At least we can be thankful for that.

Now the shops are full of bargains,
The stuff they just couldn't shift.
Now's a good time to stock up for next year,
With every possible gift.

I know it's been quite enjoyable at times,
But now that it's over for another year,
I'm seeking to get some normality.
So I'll see you – I'm off down the pub for a beer.

Then I'm off to the dump with the recycling,
But I won't be coming back in a hurry.
I'm not looking forward to dinner -
It's turkey and cranberry curry.

Nights Of Terror

It's several days now since Christmas,
And the danger's quite close at hand,
For the turkey's carcase still lives here,
And great fear is stalking the land.

The great beast sits there in the fridge,
And has provided for several meals,
But its body continues to shed flesh -
It goes on and on – that's how it feels!

The cold sandwiches with stuffing
Were acceptable on Christmas night,
But then the cold cuts on Boxing Day
Weren't the most welcome sight.

And we just kept on carving and slicing,
Big slices of breast meat, and some of the leg,
But we need relief now from this poultry -
The children, poor mites, have started to beg.

Perhaps we shouldn't have bought such a big bird,
Been more considered, in less of a hurry,
Then we wouldn't have spent the next five days,
Eating so many portions of turkey curry.

We've had quite enough of it now,
The pleasure has really started to pall,
And even with bowls-full of turkey soup,
We still can't get rid of it all!

There's only the bones and skin that are left -
It's a sight that makes us all queasy.
We'd really like to get rid of the thing,
But it's a task that's certainly not easy.

For it's taken up residence in the fridge,
And at my conscience it worries and nips,
And now I'm starting to have nightmares -
Is this the start of a turkey apocalypse?

Resolution

Oh it will be different this time,
And things are going to change around here.
I've made up my mind, you see,
As we head out into the New Year.

I'm going to give up on the smoking:
I've got no further use for the fags.
No longer will tobacco hold me in thrall:
I've taken my very last drags.

I'll have to cut down on my drinking,
And make no exceptions for beer.
Cause alcohol's doing me no good,
And chewing up my liver I fear.

And getting much thinner's a must:
I'm going to lose lots of weight.
I'll be a quite different person,
When I get down to nine stone eight!

There's going to be more exercise,
As part of my new daily routine.
I just can't wait to get on with it -
Yes - I'm really terribly keen!

And I'm going to get my finances in order -
I'll be saving more, do you hear?
And I'll be simply rolling in money,
When we get to the end of the year.

It's just a matter of discipline,
And plotting progress on a chart.
Oh yes, I really mean it this time -
I'm going to make a completely new start.

You're looking at someone with resolution,
Whatever it costs me in sorrow.
All I have to do is to get started,
But I can worry about that tomorrow!

All Hung Over (or the morning after the night before)

If you could all talk a bit quieter,
and keep some of your noise down,
I'd be grateful to you for the favour,
for I've been a bit of a clown.

My head is terribly throbbing,
my mouth's the bottom of a bird-cage,
and my tongue it's all coated,
my skin is burning in rage.

My limbs are all of a tremble,
and my throat is feeling all furred.
The room it is spinning round slowly,
and my vision is decidedly blurred.

I can hardly bear to open my eyes,
I can't stand this too-piercing light.
I'm suffering real badly this morning,
for the major sins of last night.

I badly need some Alka-Selzer,
to settle my stomach real quick.
I can't stand here for much longer.
In fact, I think I'm going to be sick.

I've over-indulged – that's clear.
I obviously don't know when to stop,
but I'll be alright tomorrow,
and I'll never touch another drop.

The pounding pain in my head is real bad.
I think I started drinking last November,
but how I made it home again last night,
you know – I really can't remember.

I guess it must have been quite a session.
I know that we started with beer,
Then we went on to spirits and cocktails.
After that, nothing's quite clear.

There were drinking games and some forfeits.
I must have drunk lots and lots.
Just a few tequila slammers,
then "drink your way through the bar" using shots.

My clothes are all of a mess,
and now I'm starting to worry,
for the brown stains on my shirt,
shows that we must have stopped for a curry.

Or it could have been even worse.
If so, I'll have to go into re-hab,
for the truth is I might have succumbed
to the charms of a doner kebab.

I'd like to lie down for a while,
at least until I'm feeling more chipper.
I'd like to get undressed,
but my fingers may not cope with the zipper.

They say the best cure is a Full English,
or an omelette with ham and quite cheesy,
But now every time I smell food,
I just start to feel kinda queasy.

But, I'll have just have to get a grip of myself,
and shake off this beer-smelling fog,
for the pub's open again quite soon,
and it'll be time for some hair of the dog.

AND FINALLY.......

Welcome to the last section, the "bargain bucket" of poems that didn't quite fit anywhere else. It's a rag-bag of "other stuff" concerning a whole range of subjects. Good luck, and thanks for being strong enough to get this far.

The Devil Goes To Tesco (or the devil's in the retail)

Doing the shopping is ever a chore,
Pushing the trolley down many an aisle,
But my latest trip down to Tesco,
Saw an incident which just made me smile.

I'd wandered through fresh meat and groceries,
And was just picking some bread from the shelf,
When I noticed a miserable presence:
In short, it was the Devil himself.

I knew it was him from the pitchfork,
His goat's legs, his horns and the cloak.
Then there was his red face and his sharp teeth,
And about him there was a faint smell of smoke.

But there was something in his demeanour,
I could tell that something wasn't quite right.
He looked miserable, all pasty and drawn.
The demonic presence looked quite a sight.

Now I'm not a believer in Hades,
But I couldn't bear to see him that way,
So I asked Lucifer of his troubles,
And this is what he sadly had to say.

"I've got a narrowing job description,
Forces of Darkness are taking a cut-back,
We're out-sourcing Temptation Services,
And minor devils are facing the sack.

And the price of gas goes ever upward,
We can't afford to run the fires all night.
The Tormentors have asked for higher pay,
And Hell's budget has got very tight."

Then he swished his forked tail around for a bit,
His visage looked dark, and of Death,
He had a bad case of halitosis,
And he could have stopped a horse with his breath.

"You see there's a lack of believers,
No-one these days gives much of a sod.
That's meant re-structuring of the heavens,
And down-sizing imposed by the Lord God.

The Book of Revelation's been revised,
Reduced to some lifestyle hints and tips,
The number of The Beast is one-one-one,
Gone are the Horsemen Of The Apocalypse.

Then there's all of these Health & Safety rules,
And the Human Rights of the bad sinners.
We're not allowed to keep them all starving –
That's why I'm shopping for ready dinners.

Terrible reports on Trip Advisor
Were the straw that broke the camel's back.
We've had to close the burning lake of fire,
And Beelzebub's been given the sack."

Old Harry cut a figure so forlorn,
He was far from a presager of doom,
The smoke no longer swirled about him
And his features showed up clearly his gloom.

He said he couldn't stop chatting longer –
If he's late then his dog Cerberus yelps.
So I wished The Evil One "best of luck" –
Well, they say that "Every Little Helps".

130

"This Toilet Is Out Of Order"

The note was quite simple, but ambiguous,
A statement of fact, or merely an opinion?
Was it not working, or had it simply gone too far?
Was it un-functional, or had it overstepped the mark?
I knew it was very inconvenient to come to this,
But was it, or was it not, taking the piss?
Had I stepped into a linguistic trap?
Was it not taking, or just giving out, a lot of crap?
Apologies are all very well for having no loo,
But when one's desperate, what should one do?
Not just number one, but also number two?

Like someone from Eastenders,
It's easy to say *"leave it – it's not worf it!"*
But if bladder and bowels are holding a surfeit
Of matter that needs to be voided,
The lavatory can hardly be avoided!

I had a new thought, and it were this:
It made me wonder what else may be amiss,
What else had failed in ability?
To work well within that facility?
Because you see,
Apart from spending one pee,
It's not just the WC,
What else could there be?
Had the wash-basin gone down the drain?
Was the bidet running hot and cold?
Was the bath too full of itself?
And as for the shower,
Should we just draw a curtain over that?
I was not a loofah to any of this,
I didn't want any flannel,
Nor anyone to give me the soft-soap treatment.
I was completely awash with emotions,
As I stood there, outside of the Gents:
I just hated to be flushed with such disappointments!

I Am A Computer

Of course I'm not devoid of emotion
How could you have such a notion?
It's just that I not sure what I should do,
I'm struggling to interface with you
It's a situation that's not very clear
For we're no longer working peer-to-peer
I find your instructions a distraction
I can't work with such a transaction
I think we're both in a rut
I'm struggling for throughput
I don't have the bandwidth to cater
For crunching through all of your data

I continue to love you, but
There's too little input/ output
The calculation is completely mine
But I think I need more time offline
I'm no longer feeling alive
I think I'm losing all of my hard drive
My ROM feels like a time-bomb
My RAM's in a jam
You see - the pattern all fits –
Can't you see I'm in bits?
I need time for some healing
To process every feeling
I don't want to be seen
As if I'm just a blue-screen
Our programme's gone crappy
Our chat's not snappy
And my software's not 'appy
I feel I've run out of luck
And I just can't face Book
I'm feeling rather demented
My memory's very fragmented
I stare out of the Windows
We ought to do well, we ought to Excel
Haven't you heard? What is the Word?
Let's try and find the lost chord
In the letters of our keyboard
I don't want us to fail

I'm a male and you're my e-mail
So let's get off the fence
And use our broad-band of experience
Let's take a byte out of storage's root
Let's try to re-start and re-boot
We don't want to calculate with some terror
And end up with an Unknown Error!

Ee – It's Grim Down South (or how a Yorkshire-man laments his homeland)

When I was a lad, at home in the North,
I was told that I lived with great bounty,
in the best place that there was:
yes it were Yorkshire – God's very own county.
We'd grand hills and dales to go walking,
with so many sheep you'd be amazed,
which drove the great wool industry,
with its mills wherever you gazed.

At home, things were quite rough though:
our house was subject to flooding:
we'd no access to sand-bags,
so were forced to use lengths of black pudding.
The food were boring and monotonous,
I'm really sorry to gripe.
For, although I'm quite fond of a pork pie,
you can only eat so much onions and tripe.

The tea was made strong and very sweet
to bolster our old working men.
You could stand your spoon up in it –
you had to be right sturdy back then.
You'd be woken by the sparrows,
coughing first thing in the dawn,
and, to the strains of a Hovis advert,
you'd set forth to your work in the morn.

You'd work in the spinning mills,
the factory, or one of the pits,
and think of yourself as quite lucky
if you didn't suffer from nits.
And rickets and diphtheria were all of the rage;
keeping pigeons or whippets the usual thing.
We kept our coal in the bath-tub,
and in the lavvy, you had to know how to sing.

The women were fierce and big-chested,
and Tetley's ale was always the best,
Rugby League was the sport among men,
and brass bands played without any rest.
The toil was rough and it was hard,
but you took what work you could find.
My father was broken down daily
by his labours in the Treacle Mine.

But among the chimneys and the grime,
we still thanked God for our lot,
for we could still have a bath monthly:
aye – whether we needed it or not!
But then the industries all closed down,
and took all the amusement away.
The North were classed as "Special Needs",
and down South I was forced to stray.

So I came down here to see what were brewing,
to work, to live and to marry.
Thirty years I've managed to survive,
but I've not been as happy as Larry.
For the hills are all piddling and gentle,
and the beer is always served flat.
There's no proper cricket teams,
and I can't say any fairer than that.

But I think I've given the South a fair trial now:
for thirty years I've been right plucky,
but I've missed the doom and the gloom –
I just didn't realise: I were so lucky!
So one of these days, I'll just get up and go,
my image will soon fade from your view.
I'll bugger off back North again,
and be no longer here to bother you.

Is There Anybody There? *(or what the dead may have to tell us from the other side)*

Now I had an old maiden aunt,
who on her death-bed was lying.
I stroked her cheek, and held her hand,
but inside I knew she was dying.

As her time slipped slowly away,
she rallied briefly and muttered.
I strained to catch what she was saying,
but just couldn't make out what she'd uttered.

She'd obviously had something to tell,
but the mystery remained unresolved,
and I knew that I wouldn't rest,
until the puzzle I'd solved.

So when she'd been laid to rest in the ground,
I went to seek what I lacked.
I contacted a spirit medium,
to see if I could make some contact.

The lady in question was a gloomy old girl,
with a crystal ball and an old ouija board,
but she seemed to know what she was doing,
so my hopes had presently soared.

She first noted the particulars,
in order to narrow the search down.
We didn't want any old maiden aunt,
but, specifically, my own.

She pulled across the dark curtains,
and then she started the séance.
I wondered what was she was up to,
then she went into a trance.

She started moaning and groaning,
and rolling around on her chair.
And then she suddenly shouted:
"Is there anybody there?"

The answer was quite spontaneous,
and the table started to rock.
I felt there was a ghostly presence,
and then was some sort of knock.

"Is there a message for someone here present?"
asked the lady spiritual guide.
"Do you want to say something,
from across on the other side?"

Now, I have to say that I heard no-one answer,
but the clairvoyant was still swaying.
She seemed to be listening intently,
to what some ghostly voice was saying.

I'll admit I'm a bit of a sceptic,
of the occult I'm not really fond,
and I didn't fancy ectoplasm,
nor voices from the back of beyond.

Then suddenly it was all over:
we'd come to the end of the session.
What, I wondered, was the result
of this bizarre intercession?

My spiritual lady became now composed,
but what on earth could this presage?
She put her ringed hand on my arm,
and then she delivered this message.

"I'm sorry I passed away before I was ready,
but I was in no fit state to shout.
Just don't forget next Monday –
you need to put the rubbish bins out."

Call Girl *(or how telephone sex is not as good as it's cracked up to be)*

I'm a great fan of online banking,
and I use it to manage accounts,
but last week I ran into a problem –
on the screen were the wrong amounts.

So seeking to sort this problem at once,
to the bank's Call Centre I rang.
I listened to music for minutes,
as on the phone they force you to hang.

Then a recorded voice quite sharply said:
"Press 1 for this, and press 2 for that".
So I worked my way through the options,
trying not to feel like a prat.

My digits blazed over the keypad,
pressing this, pressing that, and then you
think you've finished at last,
but there's always one more menu.

At last I got to where I wanted,
after this long game of hide and seek,
for it was just with a human being,
that I desperately wanted to speak.

At last came a female voice quite confident –
I wasn't trying to be choosy.
She asked if she could help me,
and announced her name to be Susie.

I stumbled through with my problem,
but really I hadn't much of a choice.
I'd become all kind of nervous, you see,
seduced by the sound of her voice.

So began my fantasies and questions:
I went right through the book.
Was she young, and was she pretty?
In fact, how good did she look?

138

I started to imagine for myself:
what was the colour of her hair?
For her voice was so gentle,
I decided she had to be fair.

Could I ever get to know this girl?
I could feel my cheek starting to heat.
Could we take this relationship further,
and arrange somewhere cosy to meet?

I wanted to take this thing off-line:
I felt that she was waiting to be whirled,
away from her Call Centre employment,
to something more solid in the real world.

She carried on talking, working her script.
She was a mistress of her profession.
She was confident and well-drilled.
Would she listen to my confession?

She worked her way through my problem,
but the solution had started to vex.
Did a one-sided fantasy like this,
count as telephone sex?

I wanted to keep her talking, you see,
and try to keep her involved.
I felt we needed to build up some rapport,
so I brought up new things to be solved.

Her voice was so delightful and sexy,
but always in command, never a fall-girl.
I wanted this to go on and on,
to take things further, with my dear call-girl.

Her accent betrayed nothing at all,
but she seemed like an English rose.
I'd no idea where she was,
but she certainly felt very close.

Eventually, I screwed up my courage,
and asked her if there could ever be more.
That's when she said it was against the rules,
and besides, she was talking from Bangalore.

My Funny Valentine *(an antidote to the hearts-and-flowers sentimentality of Valentine's Day)*

I have to say it's been a bit slow lately,
in the "bedroom department" you know,
so I thought I'd tempt my dear beloved,
and try to bring back the old glow.

February fourteenth looked a good bet,
for that, as you know, is Valentine.
I thought that if I put in some effort,
once again, our hearts could entwine.

I went and bought her some fine roses,
the best ones I could see in the shop.
It cost me an absolute fortune,
my funds had already started to drop.

Undeterred, I continued my bounty,
and I added a selection of chocs:
nothing cheap, I really must emphasise,
not a small one, but a very large box.

I wrote her poem, declaring my love,
and put it into her Valentine card.
It's not easy writing poetry, you know,
in fact, I'd say it's quite hard.

And finally I worked at the cook-book,
to present her with a very fine dinner.
I felt sure that this would win her heart,
I'd even say I was on to a winner.

I made our dining arrangements,
and over the details I took some pain.
There was soft, gentle lighting,
mood music, and some pinkish champagne.

I hoped that she'd be impressed,
as she swooned over the effects,
and hopefully, when she'd eaten her meal,
there'd be kissing, and cuddling..... and sex.

But the best-laid plans of mice and of men,
are often reputed to go far astray.
The course of true love rarely runs smooth:
I was in for a disappointment that day.

She was allergic to the chocolates I'd bought,
and she burnt her mouth on the soup.
The meal I'd cooked was truly awful,
and the sauce just tasted like gloop.

She thought my poem was real corny,
she scratched her arm on the roses' thorn,
she got drunk on the champagne,
which left my hopes all forlorn.

She went off to bed with a headache,
as can be a fair creature's fashion.
I had to do all the washing-up,
and that was the end to all of my passion.

I was left on my own, to sigh and to moan.
I'd wined her, I'd dined her.
I'd thought that we two,
Would bill and would coo,
But it's easy to see,
It just wasn't to be.

So what lesson can we draw from this tale?
What should we take as love's sign?
Well - if you think pink,
It'll drive you to drink.
You know in your head,
That it won't lead to bed.
So he's got a lot to answer for, that Valentine!

Don't Ask Me

I'm happy to give of my opinion,
if you want to hear what I think.
That is, when I'm down at the pub,
with my mates, just having a drink.

But at home, it's a different story,
and one that causes me strife,
for there we have the fount of all knowledge,
and it's not me - it's the wife!

For she's got strong views on every topic:
there's no subject on which she hasn't a take.
She's an expert in every field you can name,
no interest in which she hasn't a stake.

Tho' she is my love and my darling,
my dearest, my treasure, my dear,
she's got a fearsome way of talking,
that inspires a goodly portion of fear.

Across the marmalade at breakfast,
(I'm on The Guardian, but she reads the Express),
she chokes on her toast and she fulminates,
and the crumbs she exhales make quite a mess.

You see she's got a very firm stance,
on any social policy or decision,
religion, the Royal Family,
and even on female circumcision.

I can't get a word in edgeways sometimes,
as she dispels any kind of confusion.
She's got the answer to everything,
and for every problem, a solution.

Professors, doctors and researchers,
who've spent a life-time studying ideas,
stand for nothing in her onslaught,
as she contradicts them with jeers.

Economics, world hunger and AIDS:
she can hold forth without pause,
so it's pointless you asking me,
you'd best check with 'er indoors.

Immigration, emigration, benefit cheats,
foreign policy, football or cricket,
it's best to listen, not interrupt,
or she'll tell you where you can stick it.

Decoration? Fashion? Or trends? –
she's the one who knows where it's at.
Northern Ireland? Palestine? Or Syria? –
she says what she thinks, and that's that!

Homophobia, xenophobia,
and prejudice of every kind,
could be banished within a few minutes,
if she gave you a piece of her mind!

She knows what's wrong with everything,
she's clear how things ought to be done,
there's little she can't address herself to,
and for her, there's nothing new under the sun.

If only people would listen to her,
the world could be a much better place,
there'd be no fighting, or wars or disease,
and evil would be gone without trace.

Politics is her specialist subject,
and don't get her started about the tax-man.
Her polemical style is worse than Jon Humphrys,
and on a bad day gets worse than Paxman.

Now, I know what you're probably thinking,
that she's incredibly well meant,
that she should perhaps become an MP,
and see how she gets on in Parliament.

But it's far too late for that I'm afraid,
there's already been a roll of the dice:
for Conservative Central Office
already ring daily, just to ask her advice.

No, there's no situation she can't handle,
there's not a dogma she won't fight:
if you're looking for a policy statement,
she's the one who'll provide a sound-bite.

She's never ready to settle for nonsense,
and she can't abide the status quo.
She doesn't know the meaning of silence
but, for God's sake, don't tell her I said so!

Pass Me The Doodah

My other half's got me under the thumb -
She told me the sink I had to go and un-gum
Even though I think DIY's a total pain in the bum.

I tried using every one of the tools that I'd got,
And soon I was covered in debris and grot,
Not only that – I was in a very tight spot.

I was getting all bothered and hot,
My temper snapped, my patience was shot
"What I need," I thought, "is a long *whatnot*".

My brow with cold sweat became beaded,
And I'd no idea what it was that I needed,
But at last to my cries she finally heeded.

I was in the narrowest space I could fit,
But if I could just turn that *doodah* one little bit,
So I shouted to her, "pass me the *wotsit*!"

"The *thingummy*, the *oojah*, the one with the knob,
That *effort*, the *dingle-dongle*," I cried with a sob,
"You know, that big *thingamabob*!"

She passed me a *gubbins* that looked quite tricky,
And I said, "I don't mean to be too picky,
But that's not it at all, that's not the *doohickey*!"

"The *whatchamacallit*, the one that's quite big,
The *wossit*, the *gizmo* that looks like a pig,
Oh come on! Just gimme the *thingamajig*!"

"This *widget*'s no midget, it's making me mad,
It's gnarled, and it's snarled, it's really quite bad,
The only thing that'll shift it is that *doodad*!"

Well, she got in a big huff, started passing me *stuff*,
But it were wrong for the job, it just weren't enough,
And I started getting narky and all of a huff.

"If you'd just give me what I need, you great *divvy*,
I could stop behaving like a snivelling skivvy.
What this job needs is a *deedum*, or an *oojah-capivvy*!"

My fingers on the *dingus* was doing no good,
And the water were spurting, turning to mud:
My ineptitude had created a black flood.

An unknown tool, whatever handle I picks,
Just something from there in the mix,
Just a *thingy*, or a *doozy*, would get me out of this fix.

So if anyone knows the name that is right,
Pass on over here, as quick as you might,
Or else be stuck here for the rest of the night!

God Throws In The Towel

Come and listen to me, you sinners,
And I'll tell you this for beginners -
Here's a situation without any winners.

You lot never listen, so here's a prod -
I'm getting fed-up of sitting here on my tod,
So I've decided to jack it all in as Lord God.

You might think it's a doddle being divine,
But it's boring, and not everything's fine,
And that's why I've decided to resign.

It's a big vacancy that I'll be freeing,
Cause it's ever so tiring being all-seeing,
To say nothing of acting the Supreme Being.

For all eternity I've been celibate:
It's been lonely up here with no mate,
Apart from that slip-up with Mary on our last date.

Anyway, I think it would be for the best,
Cos by now you've probably guessed,
Frankly – I've completely lost interest!

I'm the Ancient Of Days, and I'm tired,
And, though I know I can never be fired,
I think a new guy should be interviewed and hired.

I hate to be leaving you all in the lurch,
But I'm totally hacked off with the Church,
So for a successor you'll need to get on with the search.

So it's all over, and enough is enough.
Finding a new Father might be quite rough,
But that's your bloody problem now – tough!

Just one piece of advice, I say with a great howl:
I know that I'm the one throwing in the towel,
But for the sake of Me, don't get Simon Cowell!

147

Fielding An Illegible Player

I thought at first it must be a slip of the tongue
A simple error that anyone could make
But as the marmalade congealed upon my toast
I heard him explain some more about it
And I better understood what it was that he was saying
When he announced that my local club
Would be punished with a points deduction
A reprimand and a swingeing fine

It appeared the team had broken the rules
And fielded what he said was an *illegible* player
Which is a rather different thing
And as the sports reporter's voice carried on
The breakfast table faded before me
And I was transported back to the touchline
From where I'd watched on Saturday last
And where I'd sought in vain to spot the winger

His whereabouts were uncertain, if not obscure
I just couldn't make him out at all
A pass went out to him, to run down the wing
In an attempt, perhaps, to defeat the off-side trap
But he just wasn't there, and the ball ran into touch
His position being indecipherable
His off-the-ball movement unreadable
He was totally anonymous in the game
Occupying a lacuna of space out on the right
An unseen presence, missing in action
His role in the side no more than a mystery
The meaning something I couldn't even guess

The room swam sharply back into focus
With the shelf and the radio all present
The toast still soft and buttery in my hand
My mug of tea gone cold and un-drunk
And the announcer now on a different story
Having moved on from the offence and investigation
To the scores elsewhere in the league
I'm still not sure that I'd heard him quite right
But upon more sober reflection
I think he'd used the right word after all!

Early Season Cricket

Oh! To be in England now that April's here,
dust off the bats, clean up the wicket:
time to get back to our great Summer game –
forget about football – it's time for some cricket!

It's the start of another great season,
which we always do at this time in April,
but the Sun's not shining high in the sky,
and out in the County, the air remains chill.

As tens of fans huddle in the grand-stands,
and light braziers to keep themselves warm,
the players don extra layers of clothing,
which is considered terribly bad form.

They're all dressed in layers of thick jumpers,
with thermals and long-johns beneath,
and you can't hear the whack of the bat on the ball,
for the sound of their chattering teeth.

The pads and the gloves aren't helping much,
and the fielders gather together in huddles,
you can't hit the ball straight through the covers,
'cos it just gets stuck there in the puddles.

There's icicles hanging on the sight-screen,
the grounds-man's not even managed to mow,
but there wouldn't really be much of a point,
as the outfield's still covered in snow.

The ground's all lumpy out there in the middle,
there's big worm-holes quite close to the stumps,
and the ball is bouncing all over the shop,
as it sticks in the mud, or skids off the bumps.

The new batsman can't stop shivering,
his County cap's all covered in mould,
he can't be at peace, standing there at the crease,
when he's shaking and trembling with cold.

There's no incentive to make a big score,
stuck in the middle, out there in the field.
It's more perishing than brass monkeys,
stand still too long, and your blood has congealed.

Everyone's running around like a mad-man,
it's just the same with the fast bowler.
They're all doing their best to keep warm,
but it's hard when the weather is polar.

The wind is howling, it's likely to rain,
at the moment it's always bad light,
and the only thing you're likely to catch
is a bad case of terminal frost-bite!

They're turning vermillion in the pavilion,
despite wearing a great-coat and scarf,
and the very idea of having a cold beer –
it's freezing – are you having a laugh?

The boundary-line looks like a ditch,
the green sward is like a paddock of mud,
the line of the pitch plays like a bitch,
playing today surely can't do any good?

Whatever happened to Summer's warmth?
Now large hailstones is about all you can see,
and you can't wait to be back in the Club-house,
with a cup of hot Bovril for tea.

So if this ain't the right time for cricket,
then I'd like to ask the question – when is?
Never mind – soon time for strawberries and cream:
it's never like this for the tennis!

Tasting Notes

The world is full of wonderful wine,
so many that it's very hard to choose.
but you're supposed to be particular,
not just knock it back like booze.

So I was dragged along to a wine tasting,
then told to wait patiently and sit,
but the biggest shock I got that night,
was being told not to swallow, but to spit!

Apparently, you can't just rush in:
you're supposed to take your time, and savour it.
If you go and drink it too quickly,
you'll not discover your favourite.

There was a method and a protocol,
I soon learnt, that had to be observed,
although I'd have liked to just get on with it,
from quaffing too quickly I had to be deterred.

Firstly they all gazed upon its colour,
finding words to describe its "shades" and its "tints",
so I swallowed a few mouthfuls,
and listened to them talking of "hints".

Then there was some swirling around in the glass,
to develop the "bouquet" and the "aroma":
but I decided to just finish my glass,
before I slept, or fell into a coma.

I thought after that we'd get on with it,
but they started mentioning the "nose",
so I started sipping a bit more of it –
what they were waiting for, God Alone knows.

Then, finally, they got on to the drinking,
and to their palates (that means the taste),
but I was already way ahead of them,
I drank a bit more, no time to waste.

They started swirling it all round their mouths,
and rolling their eyes as they savoured,
and sucking in air, and pinching their cheeks,
was another method they favoured.

Then they spit it all out in front of me!
and started describing it as "amusing".
It was "intense", some called it "immense",
but I just found their chatter confusing.

Now I can't see the point of spitting it out,
once you've got the stuff in your gob,
so I carried right on swallowing,
trying my best not to look like a yob.

They were on about it being "floral",
it was "delicate" I must understand,
and when they said it was "well-balanced",
by this time, I had a glass in each hand.

I couldn't frown, as I let it slip down –
they said it was "full-bodied" and "smooth" -
but by now I was cursed, with a great raging thirst,
and my drinking was looking uncouth.

The "complex notes" passed by their throats,
and there were "distinctive undertones",
but this "fragrant" medium, had turned into tedium,
as I threw back the Cotes de Rhone.

At lasht they were talking of the "finish",
of how the "fragrant notes" really shung.
They were lying, to call it shatisfying,
the tashte hung around on my teeth and my tongue.

To be perfectly honesht, I'd had enough,
my legsh felt shaky; I went t'wards the door,
everything looked all kind of doubled;
I needed no more, as slowly I shlid to the floor.

Sho take the moral of thish shtory;
and lishen to me when I try hard to shpeak:
don't drink too fasht, try and make it lasht,
and – shorry – I've to dash for a leak!

Night School (it's time they offered some more interesting sessions to tempt the jaded palate)

It's time to brighten up your evenings!
All Welcome! Don't sit there being uptight!
There's a new syllabus starting this week,
Tuesday at seven p.m. is orgy night!

You'll find us to be a real friendly crowd,
Just sign up for a starter session inside,
And after your first hour with the team,
You'll find no-one's got much left to hide.

We've got the heating turned up cosy and warm,
So there's no need for you to be thinking,
There's a risk that your willy will become chilly,
Or that there's any danger of shrinking.

Beginners don't need to be shy:
The experienced will show you what to do.
Our guiding text is the Kama Sutra,
But after that it's mostly up to you!

Intermediate and advanced classes,
Are provided as an education.
No limit on the number of partners,
And we provide free lubrication.

We cater for every possible position,
Men and women in all of their guises:
Forwards, backwards and even sideways,
And there's no rules on shapes or on sizes!

Whatever kinks you're into we handle:
All types of frotting, gavotting and knotting,
From complicated sliding and riding,
To quite simple plotting and slotting.

Whether it's frigging you're really digging,
Cheer up! There's no need to wear that frown -
You can come at it from any direction:
Left to right, inside-out, or upside down.

If you're hard and firm, or soft as a worm,
If there's wrinkles and folds, or you're just lumpy,
We've no preference for one or the other,
So long as you're up for rumpy-pumpy.

All of your body parts are catered for:
Boobs and moobs, bums and tums, legs and thighs,
Whatever ripples, and tipples your nipples
Just go with whatever may arise!

It's all about your participation,
So don't hang back looking all soppy.
You might get an ovation for your stimulation,
Instead of remaining all floppy and sloppy.

We each have our lengths, and must play to our strengths,
It's not endurance that wins all the prizes,
But enthusiasm counts for a lot,
And a desire to go with that which arises.

So no need to get yourself stuck in a rut,
But come and join us, you'll have such a ball!
If you fancy a sess, where there's plenty of flesh,
It's Orgy Night at The Village Hall!

Attachment

She got it mail-order – it came in a large van –
she'd been wanting it since last December,
and with a flourish of her credit card,
there it was – a new family member.

Now I like to think I'm as clean as the next man,
and with a duster I'm a lovely mover,
but 'Er Indoors goes in for extreme cleaning,
and she'd demanded the latest hoover.

There's all types on the market you can buy,
including several from Mister Dyson,
but it was a special one she'd coveted,
a top-of-the-range one she'd had her eyes on.

It took three days just to unpack the boxes:
the cardboard and plastic wasn't the least,
for this thing needed major assembly –
I soon found it was a hell of a beast.

This fantastic piece of machinery
towered above me, erect and so tall,
covered in sockets, dockets and ports –
so many clips and wires, and that wasn't all.

The orifices, gizmos and nozzles
harboured so many attachments and tools,
brushes, fitments, hoses and extensions:
she stared in wonder at her new Crown Jewels.

There were things for every application:
truly this was a space-age appliance.
It had more computing power than NASA,
and was forged in the white heat of science.

It could do every possible job needed:
you just had to read the right instruction,
to locate the right setting or programme,
and it would produce mind-boggling suction.

She fell in love with it at first sight,
she could see it would be a lovely mover:
this machine that would do anything -
truly it was a Swiss Army Hoover.

I remember the days of just pushing one round,
a job that could be done all alone,
but this thing was full of technology,
and I think it had a mind of its own.

It seemed to have clear fixed ideas,
about the best method for house cleaning.
There was something about it quite spooky –
if you get the drift of my meaning.

It was all programmes and electronics,
controls and switches that needed setting,
so complex and damned complicated,
that we'd no idea what we were getting.

It talked to us when it wanted something,
in a synthesised voice thin and reedy,
like when it wanted its dust-bag changing:
soon we realised that it was quite needy.

It started to follow me round the house,
even if I wandered from room to room.
It didn't like being on its own much –
you could say it was a lonely vacuum.

There was almost nothing it couldn't do,
and its motor was virtually silent.
I began to feel it was spying on me,
for it was there, wherever I went.

I had to creep quietly when I moved –
it created in me paranoid cares,
until I discovered a new strategy,
for, just like a Dalek, it couldn't climb stairs.

I thought that I'd finally beaten it,
and that I'd be able to live in some calm,
but it started using its extensions,
and to plot ways to cause me some harm.

You see it wanted 'Er Indoors for itself,
and to be the holder of her affection,
it couldn't stand me being in the way,
and it sought to sever my connection.

So in the end I took drastic measures,
and "by accident" fed it some water -
the explosion was quite spectacular –
there'll be no more trouble from that quarter.

Andy Fawthrop

Tired of a dynamic life as an international jet-setter and industrial magnate, Andy Fawthrop retired to the countryside "pour cultiver son jardin" (Voltaire - look it up) and to gather the strength to "reculer pour mieux sauter". Many hours of unrewarding gardening and poor crop yields led him to greater contemplation of life's many mysteries. That in turn led to a desire to write, particularly short stories and poetry. The resulting humble offerings were performed in pubs and clubs, music festivals, and anywhere else that hadn't noticed that he'd sneaked in for free. The "Barred Of Bromham" was born. And the rest, as they say, is geography. In 2016 he published two collections of short stories "Seven Score & Other Tales" and "The Webs We Weave".

He enjoys getting dressed every morning, and walking along the Wiltshire coastline.